Crisis Counseling

Creative Pastoral Care and Counseling Series
  Editor: Howard J. Clinebell, Jr.
  Associate Editor: Howard W. Stone

Crisis Counseling

Howard W. Stone

Fortress Press Philadelphia

COPYRIGHT © 1976 BY FORTRESS PRESS

Fourth printing 1983

Library of Congress Catalog Card Number 75-13047
ISBN 0-8006-0553-5

545D83   Printed in the United States of America   1-553

For Karen and Christine

Contents

Series Foreword

Let me share with you some of the hopes that are in the minds of those of us who helped to develop this series— hopes that relate directly to you as the reader. It is our desire and expectation that these books will be of help to you in developing better working tools as a minister-counselor. We hope that they will do this by encouraging your own creativity in developing more effective methods and programs for helping people live life more fully. It is our intention in this series to affirm the many things you have going for you as a minister in helping troubled persons—the many assets and resources from your religious heritage, your role as the leader of a congregation, and your unique relationship to individuals and families throughout the life cycle. We hope to help you reaffirm the *power of the pastoral* by the use of fresh models and methods in your ministry.

The aim of the series is not to be comprehensive with respect to topics but rather to bring innovative approaches to some major types of counseling. Although the books are practice-oriented, they also provide a solid foundation of theological and psychological insights. They are written primarily for ministers (and those preparing for the ministry), but we hope that they will also prove useful to other counselors who are interested in the crucial role of spiritual and value issues in all helping relationships. In addition we hope that the series will be useful in seminary courses, clergy support groups, continuing education workshops, and lay befriender training.

This is a period of rich new developments in counseling and psychotherapy. The time is ripe for a flowering of creative methods and insights in pastoral care and counseling. Our expectation is that this series will stimulate grass roots creativity as innovative methods and programs come alive for you. Some of the major thrusts that will be discussed in this series include a new awareness of the unique contributions of the theologically trained counselor, the liberating power of the human potentials orientation, an appreciation of the pastoral-care function of the ministering congregation, the importance of humanizing systems and institutions as well as close relationships, the importance of pastoral *care* (and not just counseling), the many opportunities for caring ministries throughout the life cycle, the deep changes in male-female relationships, and the new psychotherapies —for example, gestalt therapy, transactional analysis, educative counseling, and crisis methods. Our hope is that this series will enhance your resources for your ministry to persons, by opening doorways to understanding of these creative thrusts in pastoral care and counseling.

In this volume, Howard Stone has given us a practical guide to using the new short-term helping methods called crisis counseling. These methods are good news to all counselors, particularly to busy parish pastors and other part-time counselors. The author describes these new tools, and the principles underlying them, succinctly and clearly, showing how crises can become growth opportunities.

In working with Howard Stone on this series, I have been impressed by the things that will become evident to you in these pages—his ability to go to the heart of an issue and his competency in integrating theory and practice. Also evident in these pages is his continuing involvement in both doing and teaching what he writes about—crisis counseling. This results from his work as director of the Interfaith Counseling Service in Scottsdale, Arizona.

The author's pastoral orientation makes him aware of

the strategic advantages of the minister in crisis work and of the crucial need for spiritual growth in coping constructively with crises. He presents the basic steps in crisis counseling but goes further, describing with illuminating examples how the pastor can apply these and how he or she can mobilize the congregation as a caring community for those in crises. The author then shows by case examples how the principles can be adapted in such varied crises as loss of a job, attempted suicide, unmarried pregnancy, and a child's response to moving.

Howard Stone has brought together here two rich streams —the newer insights from the mental health literature on crisis intervention and the pastoral heritage. The results will undoubtedly prove useful to anyone—layperson, minister, or other counselor—who wants to enhance his or her skills in helping human beings cope creatively with the heavy blows of life.

HOWARD J. CLINEBELL, JR.

Preface

The minister in most communities is obviously one of the key individuals for dealing with crisis. I have specifically written this book for ministers—though I am certain it will be of value to mental health professionals and laypersons as well. My hope is that the learnings from this book will further strengthen the crisis intervention of all who are called upon to counsel.

My aim is to share my understanding of the theory of crisis intervention and to detail a counseling method which can be used in managing crises. I urge the reader not to skip over the theoretical discussion in chapter 2, since in crisis intervention a solid understanding of the dynamics of crisis is necessary for effective crisis management. The purpose of the book is to bring the time-honored skills of pastoral care and counseling together with the new methods of crisis intervention that have recently emerged in the field of psychology. The cases related here, although modified to protect confidentiality, are from my own counseling ministry and that of other ministers and counselors.

As will become apparent in due course, crisis intervention has much in common with other more traditional forms of counseling, but there are also some important differences. It focuses on persons at a time in their lives when they are particularly open to the help of a caring counselor. It is a supportive rather than "uncovering" kind of therapy; the goal is not to break down defense mechanisms but to build on and develop existing strengths. It is necessarily short-term and oriented to dealing with specific present problems and concerns. All of these aspects make crisis counseling a matter of growing interest—and potential help—to parish ministers today.

I have always been interested in knowing how a particular book came to be written. Sometimes a book comes to the author in a flash of inspiration. Crisis counseling, on the contrary, evolved slowly. When I began my ministry, I felt unsure of myself while counseling people in crises; and my typical response to uncertainty and anxiety is to read, study, and try to understand. In seminary I had already developed an interest in the subject of crisis intervention. This interest increased while I was working on my doctoral dissertation at the Suicide Prevention Center in Los Angeles. Even before writing my first book, *Suicide and Grief*, an outline for the present book had begun to take shape in my mind. Since then I have been collecting ideas on crisis theory, trying new intervention methods with people I am counseling, and teaching courses in crisis intervention at the Lutheran Seminary at Philadelphia and at Arizona State University. It is from these experiences over a period of some years that the present book has grown.

I cannot in this brief preface express appreciation to every person who assisted me in the preparation of this book. Nevertheless, I would like to extend special thanks to John Landgraf for sharing his valuable insights on the subject of referral and—together with Alton Goodenberger—for reading and offering valuable criticisms of the manuscript; to my students who provided me with feedback and case histories; to Howard J. Clinebell, Jr., editor of the Creative Pastoral Care and Counseling Series, for his insightful comments; and finally to Karen Stone who helped in editing and preparing the manuscript.

1. The Minister as Crisis Counselor

I was still a "green" seminary student, poring over my books early one Wednesday evening, when I received a phone call from Sandra Chase, a woman in the Philadelphia congregation where I was serving as assistant pastor.

Sandra was nearly hysterical. She said she had to see me right away, that her seventeen-year-old son Gary had just informed her he was going to elope that weekend. She was violently opposed to the youthful marriage, but Gary was equally adamant, and they needed me to help them.

Before I had a chance to ask whether Sandra had called the pastor—I was a little scared and wanted to "pass the buck"—she told me he was out of town. Over the phone I agreed to meet with Sandra, her husband Leonard, Gary, and his girl friend Jeanne that same evening.

This was the first crisis I had ever been called upon to deal with in the role of pastor. As I drove to the Chase's home I felt for the first time the kind of fear you experience when you know other people are counting on you because you are a minister—but you don't know what you're going to do.

Both of the teen-agers were quite mature and open to negotiation. Jeanne's parents had already indicated that they would not even talk with me, but Sandra and Leonard finally decided to support the couple when they realized that the wedding was going to take place anyway, with or without their approval. But they wanted a church wedding for their son. For one with some training in the leadership of worship it was easy to help the four reach a compromise on that point. After Gary and Jeanne had returned from their elopement the church's rite for the Blessing of a Civil Marriage was performed, much like a regular wedding, and the congregation shared in the event.

The young couple came to me for several counseling sessions afterward, at which time we dealt with where they would live, finances, sex, contraception, children, and how they would deal with relatives (especially Jeanne's parents). There were some residual bad feelings; the elder Chases were particularly resentful of Jeanne's parents for "abandoning" the couple. But the church ceremony, and the willingness of most of the people involved to get together and talk, helped Jeanne and Gary get started on a good foot at a time of life which can often be exceedingly hazardous. It is possible that the successful resolution of this crisis may have helped to prevent or ameliorate future crisis.

All of us experience crises from time to time. All of us come upon those crucial moments when we have to make a decision, solve a problem, deal with a significant issue, or confront an agonizing or terrifying situation. At such times we may seek out the help of spouses, friends, colleagues, or professionals such as ministers or psychologists. In one way or another, whether the minister likes it or not, he or she is faced with crises in parishioners' lives. Crisis ministry has been part of pastoral care throughout many centuries in which Christians have learned to expect their pastors to be with them at crucial times.

A new literature and methodology, referred to as "crisis intervention," has recently emerged in the fields of psychology, psychiatry, and social work. The purpose of the present book is to blend new learnings from these mental health fields with the time-honored skills of pastoral care. The purpose is *not* to survey various methods of crisis intervention practice, nor to develop a new theory, but rather to share a particular method of intervention based upon recent theories of crisis, a method which for me makes sense theoretically and has been effective in practice.

A Brief History of the Development of Crisis Intervention

Sigmund Freud has given us an early case of the effective treatment of crisis. The famed conductor Bruno Walter, after the birth of his first child in 1906, developed partial paralysis in his right arm. Medical treatment failed to alleviate the paralysis and Walter sought out Freud, expecting the usual in-depth psychoanalysis. Instead, the treatment consisted of only six visits. Freud suggested that Walter take a vacation, then attempt to conduct even with his disability. Freud said he would assume responsibility for the success of Walter's performance. It worked! Walter had no further trouble in his long and successful career.*

Anton T. Boisen, a pioneer in the field of pastoral care and counseling, was one of the first authors to write about crisis from a religious perspective, responding to his own experiences and his observations of others in mental hospitals. His ideas about crisis first appeared in *The Exploration of the Inner World*† and more explicitly in *Religion in Crisis and Custom*.‡ For Boisen a crisis posed not only a danger but also an opportunity for spiritual and emotional growth because of the heightened emotional and intellectual processes involved in dealing with it.

Contemporary crisis intervention theory began with Erich Lindemann and Gerald Caplan, psychiatrists at the Harvard University School of Public Health. Their theory developed from Lindemann's study in 1943 of the grief responses among the survivors of the Coconut Grove fire which destroyed the famous Boston nightclub. Lindemann observed that grief is a natural and necessary reaction following a death and that there are a series of phases in the grief process.§ In 1946 Lindemann and Caplan established the Wellesley Project, a community organization for mental health

*Notes are to be found at the back of the book beginning on p. 75.

emphasizing preventive intervention. Caplan postulated that there are both adaptive and unadaptive ways of responding to emotional hazards in one's life. How adaptively a person copes with these hazards will determine whether he or she will be more likely to have emotional problems later, or will be better equipped to handle future crises. Lindemann and Caplan did not view crisis as illness, but as a normal behavioral response to a threatening situation.* The method of treatment based on their model focuses on supplementing and strengthening the individual's personal resources.

While Lindemann and Caplan were working in the area of grief as crisis, in the late fifties and early sixties, Edwin Shneidman and Norman Farberow in Los Angeles were beginning to unearth some interesting discoveries about the crisis causing or resulting from suicide. They established the Los Angeles Suicide Prevention Center, where they offered counsel to those threatening suicide, conducted research on life-threatening behavior, and greatly increased our knowledge of what happens in a crisis.

As we can see from this short history, crisis intervention is a relatively new field. There is at present a burgeoning of literature in the field, some of which is mentioned in the annotated bibliography at the end of this book. Hopefully the current interest in crisis theory will be more than a passing fashion and will develop into a competent and respectable discipline both in psychology and in pastoral care. However, it is important to stress at this point that crisis intervention is only *one* form of pastoral care, which in turn is only *one* form of ministry. We are called to encounter others not only in their moments of crisis or despair, but also in their times of hope; not only in their sadness but also in their joy.

Clarifying Terms

Crisis is defined by Webster as a "crucial time" and "a turning point in the course of anything." As used in the present context it is the term for an individual's internal reaction to an external hazard. Involved is a temporary loss of coping abilities, the tacit assumption being that the emotional dysfunction is reversible. The person in crisis is not necessarily mentally ill. He or she is simply responding emotionally to a hazardous circumstance, and if the person effectively copes with the threat, a return to prior levels of functioning will result.

There are two basic types of crisis: *developmental*, and *situational* (or *accidental*). Normal developmental crises are the predictable, though critical, experiences we all go through in the maturation process, such as the emotional turmoils attendant upon adolescence or middle age.* Situational crises are exceptional and unpredictable; they are the emotional trials and dysfunctions which result from unusual circumstances.

The aim of crisis intervention—and the aim of this book —is to help individuals deal with the latter. Situational crises might arise in connection with the loss of a job, or of a supporting person, or of a position of status and respect; an incapacitating accident, illness, or operation (such as a mastectomy); the death of a friend, relative, child, or spouse; one's own impending death; marital infidelity; severe alcoholism or drug addiction; the discovery of a handicap; an unwanted pregnancy; abortion; moving away from a situation of security; a national disaster or massive calamity such as war, depression, or hurricane; suicide; getting into trouble with the law; being drafted; sudden religious conversion; the discovery of a spouse's homosexuality; miscarriage; premature birth; loss of welfare money; entering a retirement home; parents coming to live with their married children; birth of a mongoloid child. The list could go on and on. Almost any event may be the actual precipitator of a situational crisis if it poses a serious threat to the individual.

Crisis intervention refers to a relatively new method of aiding individuals to cope with these emotionally decisive moments in their lives. It includes pastoral counseling as well as other forms of pastoral care, and all activities designed to influence the course of a particular crisis so that a return to more adaptive behavior and satisfying relationships will result, including the ability to better cope with future crises. The minister entering into the life situation of an individual or family in crisis has the dual objective of reducing, wherever possible, the impact of the crisis-precipitating event; and using the critical situation to help those affected to strengthen themselves in solving future problems by learning more effective methods of coping. A crisis calls for new action, and its challenge may stimulate new coping methods which serve to increase an individual's capacity for adapting and raise his or her level of mental and spiritual health. Crisis intervention is not just Band-Aid therapy, but *growth counseling*.

The Minister's Natural Advantages and Unique Perspective

The minister is frequently singled out as having a "natural" role for crisis intervention in contrast to other mental health professionals. Grief, for example, automatically brings the minister into involvement with the bereaved. When an individual in suffering finally seeks out the counsel of a psychiatrist or other mental health professional, it is usually because the clergy or other natural interveners, such as family and friends, have failed to relieve the distress. The minister is often among the first persons to be sought out when crises arise, and is a "natural" crisis counselor for several reasons.

For one, the pastor has a core of previously established relationships with people in the congregation. More than anyone else in the community, with the possible exception of the family doctor, he or she has cared for families during the normal developmental crises and periods of stress they encounter. Many times a minister has actually ushered a family in crisis through several previous developmental or even situational crises, and therefore has specific knowledge of how the family copes with stress. He or she may therefore be aware of methods of intervention which have been effective with these persons in the past.

Due to the minister's availability and pastoral initiative, a person coming for help will not face weeks or even months of waiting lists, medical scrutiny, or long case histories. Unlike many professionals, the minister is expected to go where the people are. He or she has always been able to schedule counseling appointments in places other than the office— particularly in the home of the persons involved. Visiting people in the hospital, on the job, and in their homes, the minister can achieve a greater depth of relationship and can learn to know people in many more ways than the average psychiatrist or psychologist can know them. A minister who observes that a family in serious crisis is not seeking help can seize the initiative, make pastoral visits, and offer assistance.

Unlike many mental health professionals who have a predominantly individualistic focus, the minister is oriented toward dealing with families and even extended families. A person in crisis is best helped by the involvement of as many "significant others" as possible. The pastor often knows the individual's family and relatives and can call on them for assistance during the crisis.

"The person in crisis," writes David K. Switzer, "is one who has begun to lose perspective, feel anxious and helpless, often depressed and worthless, frequently without hope, whose future seems to be blocked out, who even has lost sight of some of his own past. Faith . . . is a direct counterforce to the dynamics of crisis."* A minister may find it troublesome in day-to-day relationships to have people regarding him or her symbolically as God's "representative." However, to a person in crisis, this very power and authority attributed to the pastor can mean much for the restoration of the perspective and hope so desperately needed.

Howard J. Clinebell, Jr., points out that "in many cases crises confront people with the emptiness of their lives, the poverty of their relationships."* In the face of such emptiness, the minister, as the one individual in the community trained to deal with ultimate questions of meaning and value, can help the person to rediscover that even in the midst of tragedy life—lived in relationship with a loving and dependable God—has meaning.

The minister doing crisis counseling and pastoral care is unique in being able to draw upon a support group of local people within the congregation. Secular therapists have no such source of committed individuals to rely upon. Church members who call or visit persons in crisis offer not only assistance, but a sense of belonging that can offset loneliness and isolation.

A major difference between pastoral crisis intervention and counseling, and secular crisis intervention is in the perspective of the counselor. The minister treating persons in crisis may use the same crisis intervention methods as other mental health professionals, but he or she approaches them from a different point of view. The pastoral counselor finds that, in counseling with deeply troubled people or with people in crisis, questions concerning the meaning of life, death, pain, and suffering arise almost inevitably. No matter how the client depicts the problem—mental, psychiatric, interpersonal, or intrapsychic—all crises are religious at their core; they involve ultimate issues with which one must come to terms if one's life is to be fulfilling. The minister's counseling is in its final and basic concern spiritual. LeRoy Aden, a professor of pastoral theology, describes "final" in this sense as that which is ultimate from a long-term viewpoint, the end or climactic point of a process. "Basic," on the other hand, he describes as "pointing to that which is ultimate for man in the present moment, to the depth dimension of a particular moment of time."† Aden goes on to say that the minister's "final" and "basic" concerns differ from those of psychology. The minister, like any counselor, needs to deal with the client's immediate struggles; but "pastoral counseling has a different guiding image of man's plight and rescue, and therefore it often perceives in the client's verbalizations a different struggle and end-point."*

The counselor who has experienced the despair of a person who has lived an emotionally shattering childhood, suffered years of hardship and failure, and now faces another emotionally hazardous and crucial situation can capture the relevance of such theological concepts as sacrifice, sin, grace, God, apocalypse, faith, and hope.

The unique religious perspective of the pastoral counselor is brought to bear within a community of faith. The community of faith is not only a specific geographical area, or a specific congregation of believers, but a common level of humanity where the individual capacities of each person are brought out. It is not necessarily a place or a purpose, a size or a location, but a kind of experience that one has in encountering others. The community of faith is constantly attuned to the word of God in each individual situation. Bringing the word of God to a woman grieving the loss of her husband for example, may mean no more than sitting with her and holding her hand; it is not necessarily a verbal exercise. Where such community exists in a local congregation the minister receives and offers to persons in crisis the support and caring of other members of the household of faith.

It should be noted that other mental health professionals have themselves realized the importance of the religious factor in meeting the problems of living to which the pastoral counselor is especially well-equipped to respond. Carl Jung has said, "Among all my patients in the second half of life (that is to say, over thirty-five) there has not been one whose problem in the last resort was not that of finding a religious outlook on life."† Erich Fromm also recognized humankind's religious yearnings: "There is no one without a religious need, a need to have a frame of orientation and an object of devotion."* Viktor Frankl, who spent three grim years in a Nazi prison camp, emphasizes strongly the need for meaning in life: "Woe to him who saw no more sense in his life, no aim, no purpose, and therefore no point in carrying on. He was soon lost."† One of the most important things a minister can offer an individual in crisis is a relationship through which is communicated the sense that life has meaning, purpose, and hope.

There is no question but what the pastor brings to crisis intervention distinct advantages and perspectives. The fruitfulness of their application can be enhanced by his knowledge of the nature and dynamics of crisis.

2. The Dynamics of Crisis

"But Saul, still breathing threats and murder against the disciples of the Lord, went to the high priest and asked him for letters to the synagogues at Damascus, so that if he found any belonging to the Way, men or women, he might bring them bound to Jerusalem. Now as he journeyed he approached Damascus, and suddenly a light from heaven flashed about him. And he fell to the ground and heard a voice saying to him, 'Saul, Saul, why do you persecute me?' And he said, 'Who are you, Lord?' And he said, 'I am Jesus, whom you are persecuting; but rise and enter the city, and you will be told what you are to do.' The men who were traveling with him stood speechless, hearing the voice but seeing no one. Saul arose from the ground; and when his eyes were opened, he could see nothing; so they led him by the hand and brought him into Damascus. And for three days he was without sight, and neither ate nor drank " (Acts 9:1-9).

This passage from the New Testament is one of the most famous accounts in existence of a sudden religious conversion—an event which can often precipitate a crisis. Saul's experience was undoubtedly more bizarre than many conversions, resulting as it did from God's rather explicit involvement in the form of a vision. However, in spite of— or even because of—these extreme circumstances, it serves as a good example of how such an extraordinary experience can effect a crisis for the individual.

Saul's dramatic conversion, occurring as he walked along the sandy, sunbaked road outside Damascus affected him physically—when he opened his eyes "he could see nothing" and had to be led by the hand into the city. The conversion experience also affected him mentally—he questioned his old beliefs and actions, for example, his standing by at the stoning of Stephen. Indeed, Paul was changed spiritually— one of the most vigorous persecutors of Christianity became one of its most ardent promoters as he even allowed himself to be persecuted for the faith. Further, the conversion affected him emotionally, so much so that he "neither ate nor drank" for several days. The conversion of Paul caused a crisis, a turning point, in which many aspects of his life and personality were affected.

Most of us realize that crucial moments occur in our lives but we may be vague as to precisely what a crisis is. For counselors it is important to determine exactly what occurs in a situational crisis, since the methodology of crisis counseling works well only if the counselee is actually in crisis. A sound theoretical understanding is essential for effective ministry in a crisis. The purpose of this chapter, therefore, is to describe the theory of crisis—how a crisis develops and the characteristics which mark its occurrence.

How a Crisis Develops

Recalling that a crisis is an internal reaction to an external hazard, not to be confused with the precipitating event, it is helpful to think of the development of a crisis in terms of four major steps or phases (see diagram 1).

---

diagram 1

Precipitating event —> Appraisal —> Resources and coping

methods —> Crisis

The first is the stimulus or precipitating event. This is the external situation—such as death or job loss—described by theorists as an emotionally hazardous event.

The second step is the individual's particular appraisal of the situation. It is what people "make" of a precipitating event—their perception of the event as a serious threat. Involved here are not only the individual's knowledge and beliefs, ideas and expectations, but also a unique perception of the elements in the specific situation.

Each individual has his or her own way of looking at a particular event. The death of a close friend, for example, is appraised in terms of one's past relationships with the deceased and one's previous experiences with loss. The appraisal varies also with the personality of the person affected. The importance of the loss to the bereaved person, for example, determines to a great extent whether or not a crisis will develop. Thus the widow who has been deeply involved in the life of her deceased husband will perceive a greater loss than will his business associates who had only tangential relationships with him.

In the third phase of the development of a crisis, the individual's own coping methods and personal resources (such external resources as friends and relatives, minister and doctor, and such internal resources as ability to face up to and cope with new situations and problems and feelings) are used to do something about the perception of the event. The adequacy of these resources and coping methods affects the extent to which an event will be experienced as a crisis. Richard S. Lazarus states that "when the individual discovers some important motive or value is being threatened, coping activity is mobilized by virtue of this threat, by virtue of the cognition that 'My life, health, wealth, or cherished social relationships are in danger.' "* The goal of coping is the reduction or elimination of the appraised threat. The coping resources, along with the appraisal of the situation, are the two variables in the crisis process.

Finally the individual enters the crisis itself, reacting internally to the external hazard. The key to the development of a crisis is that the person's appraisal process (perception) deems the precipitating event a serious threat and the coping process does not readily resolve the threatening situation. The resulting acute crisis, most theorists and practitioners agree, usually lasts a maximum of from four to six weeks, though the after-effects of any crisis, especially grief, may continue for years.

When we talk about a crisis, therefore, we are not talking about an external event, though such an event is usually involved as a precipitator. For example, when all the employees of a small-town plant were laid off indefinitely, each person reacted to this event differently because of his or her different perception of the layoff, and according to the different coping methods and resources each possessed. Robert Biddle, who had adequate financial resources, interpersonal relationships, and internal strengths, weathered the layoff with little or no experience of a crisis. Others, like Al Daniels, lacked these resources, appraised the event as catastrophic, and went through a real crisis. Al experienced the layoff as a "slam" against his manhood; he responded by becoming irritable and autocratic at home, nearly leading to divorce. Thus two men could experience the same precipitating event in quite different ways. For one it led to severe crisis, for the other it did not.

Characteristics of Crisis

In the effort to understand what takes place in any given crisis it is important to keep in mind the various characteristics which relate to crisis and crisis intervention. For the purposes of analysis, these can be separately listed and identified. As we list them we shall also comment briefly on each.

1. Every individual has previously experienced a series of normal developmental crises in his or her life; most individuals have also experienced previous situational crises.

Until lately, the crisis state was assumed clinically but never demonstrated scientifically. Howard A. Halpern recently set out to test the hypothesis that "crisis behavior would occur in individuals in crisis situations more significantly than in individuals in non-crisis situations."* "Crisis behavior" included tiredness and exhaustion, helplessness, inadequacy, confusion, physical symptoms, anxiety, disorganization of functioning in work relationships, disorganization of family relationships, and disorganization in social activities. He tested four typical groups of people who might be expected to be in crisis: students visiting a mental health clinic, divorcees, individuals entering mental hospitals, and people in bereavement. These were compared with a control group of persons who had not recently experienced any emotionally hazardous event. The testing and validation of this hypothesis may seem simple and even unnecessary, but, as Halpern states, "Were this hypothesis not validated, the concept 'crisis' would be meaningless when applied to individuals because their behavior could not be differentiated from that of any individual selected from a non-crisis population."†

"Crisis behavior" occurred significantly more often among people in crisis than among those who were not in crisis. At the same time Halpern's study found a lack of significant difference between the various types of crisis-precipitating events. This suggests that there is considerable commonality in the behavior of people who are in crisis, though their situations may be quite diverse. It means that we can study and practice crisis intervention without having to evaluate diverse responses to the several precipitators of crisis.

2. Crises are not signs of mental illness, but are a person's "normal" reaction to an emotionally hazardous situation.

In physical disasters, such as floods or earthquakes, we are not surprised to see people experience extreme emotional disturbances; these are expected consequences. Yet when the precipitator of the crisis is not physical but emotional or relational—perhaps bereavement or divorce—there tends to be a stigma attached to the person's changed behavior. In such situations the persons affected are sometimes labeled "mentally ill."

It is important to stress that conflict and unhappiness are not necessarily synonomous with mental illness. In fact, at the appropriate time and at the appropriate place, in a "bad" situation, the existence of such conflict and unhappiness would be a sign more of health than of illness; conversely, a person who does not, for example, grieve the death of someone close is more logically to be suspect of emotional ill health.

It must be noted, however, that although persons in crisis are not necessarily mentally ill, they may experience very strong emotional reactions such as anxiety, depression, tension, panic, a personal and social sense of confusion and chaos, feelings of loss, helplessness, hopelessness, or disorganization, etc. The emotional pain can certainly lead to more serious mental distress if not resolved adaptively.

3. There is usually an outside precipitator or emotionally hazardous situation, such as death, divorce, or loss of job, which triggers the crisis; these precipitators are always situational and frequently interpersonal in nature.

As Halpern's study indicated, there was no significant difference in the quality of the upsetness occasioned by the various precipitators. However, some crisis precipitators (such as bereavement) will generally stimulate a greater quantity of upsetness than others (such as the birth of a premature child). Although the extent and duration of the upsetness may be less in some of these lesser crises, the quality of being upset will still be manifested in the same typical manner as in the case of the severe crisis precipitators.

Many writers who discuss the "causes" of emotional problems, such as those associated with divorce, tend to be overly simplistic. Clearly, not all divorced people experience the tumultous feelings usually described by these writers. Yet in crisis intervention counseling this focus on the precipitator is necessary. It is essential for both the minister and the crisis sufferer to identify the precipitating event.

In many situations awareness of the precipitator is not readily accessible to the person in distress. A fifty-six-year-old man who went to his family doctor with stomach cramps and depression, for example, did not recognize any connection between the pain and his recent discovery that his son was a homosexual. To quote Shneidman, "The crisis intervener is content (because his goals are different) to deal primarily with precipitating causes. If someone is shaking with anxiety after an earthquake, one deals with the precipitant of the anxiety and is content to mollify or reduce the intensity of the symptom which resulted from the event."*

4. In the face of an identical situation, some individuals will regard it as emotionally hazardous and experience a crisis, while others will not; there is no direct cause-and-effect relationship between the precipitator and the crisis as such.

In a crisis a breakdown of thinking occurs when the individual's mental circuits become overloaded, so to speak, and a large input of information is incompatible with the precrisis pattern of thinking about one's self, one's world, and one's interpersonal relationships. This overload of incompatible information, sometimes called "cognitive dissonance," interferes with usual ways of planning and carrying out effective behaviors.

The cognitive dissonance, which results from an individual's appraisal of the threat in a precipitator (finding out that one has terminal cancer, for example) leads the person to try first old and then new and different ways of eradicating the confusing feelings. Some individuals will respond adaptively while others will not. This is obvious to veterans with wartime experience; some soldiers become more mature and mentally healthy in combat, while others respond with "combat fatigue" or "traumatic neurosis." A crisis therefore affords the individual a chance to go one of two ways: either grow in his or her own personal maturity, or adapt poorly—possibly so poorly that he or she will have to be hospitalized.

5. An individual's appraisal or perception of the emotionally hazardous situation greatly determines whether or not a crisis will occur, and how serious it will become.

People respond differently to the same precipitator—depending on how, on the basis of their previous experience and understanding, they assess its importance for them. We spoke of this in connection with the second of the four steps or stages in the development of a crisis, about how crucial is the person's perception of the threat.

6. Most individuals in crisis perceive a loss or threatened loss of something very important to them—some source of physical, economic, interpersonal, or emotional well-being.

The loss can be that of a significant person, a love or dependency relationship, financial support, health, life, a familiar role, a sense of worthfulness, or meaning in life. The minister needs to be aware that losses do not necessarily occur only in the form of divorce or death. Significant loss can occur when an individual gets a new job or moves to a different part of the country.

When Bill was promoted from machinist to foreman he gained greater prestige in the eyes of society, better pay, and greater job security. But he lost one of the things that was most important to him—the interpersonal relationships with those who had been his colleagues. Instead of talking and cracking jokes with coequals, he now had to prod subordinates to do more work, and report them if they didn't. Bill found it difficult to do this; he was unhappy with his promotion and even talked of quitting. In handling a loss such as Bill experienced, the minister who has confronted bereavement many times can confidently adapt and then utilize methods he or she has used before to deal with this severest of all losses.

7. The greater the number and diversity of coping meth-

ods, the more likely it will be that an individual will not experience a crisis, or will not experience as severe a crisis as would an individual with a poorer set of coping skills.

A crisis will occur only when the person's early attempts at coping with the threat fail. ("Coping" refers to doing something—even if this means choosing to do nothing—to resolve the perceived threat in the precipitator.) Where traditional coping fails, disruption from the appraised threat remains and in fact increases. The individual becomes immobilized or frantically tries harder with the older coping methods which have already proved inadequate for resolving the crisis.

Think back over the number of people you know who have said in a crisis, "I just don't know what to do," or "I feel so helpless," or "I've tried everything and nothing seems to work." It is precisely because of this paralysis that a crisis has occurred. Had the individual been able to use regular coping methods and deal successfully with the perception of the event, then he or she would not have experienced a crisis.

Lazarus believes the nature of an emotional response is determined by the appraisal of the precipitator's personal significance for the individual. He postulates two possible types of appraisal: threat and non-threat.* Negative emotions result when the precipitants are appraised as threatening. Extreme negative appraisals are integral to what we define as a crisis.

Lazarus divides the appraisal processes into primary and secondary appraisal.† Primary appraisal, or perception, deals with the issue of threat or non-threat. Secondary appraisal has to do with choosing a way of coping with the perceived threat. Thus a person in crisis is one who appraises a given precipitator as extremely threatening, and who can find no effective way of coping with it.

I have found in dealing with crises that individuals will frequently come to me with a number of fairly severe situations at once. They have been handling the vexing situations with at least marginal effectiveness for a prolonged period of time without experiencing a crisis. When at last a point of exhaustion is reached, however, or the "final straw" is added—which could seem like only a minor event to some other person—he or she does not have enough strength to sustain the previously adequate coping resources and the dam bursts. In situations like this the stimulus for the crisis may sometimes appear minor to the helper (it has been said facetiously that a minor operation may be defined as an operation that happens to someone else), but it must be remembered that a crisis is always of major importance to the person experiencing it, even if the precipitator seems insignificant to others. There are, of course, some critical situations (such as death of a loved one, loss of a job, divorce) which are so commonly experienced as major upsets that they result in crises in most instances.

8. The more seriously threatening an individual's appraisal of an event, the more primitive or regressive his or her coping resources will likely be.

Persons in severe crisis are less in touch with reality. They lose all concept of time. They tend to pull away from important and need-satisfying relationships.

Concurrently, if inconsistently, the minister will often encounter a desire for a regressive, nurturing relationship. The person will often manifest considerable dependency, infantile clinging, which has a tendency to repel others and provoke rejection and isolation.

9. A result of this regression to primitive coping methods is increased suggestibility and diminished mistrust, leading to what is referred to as "heightened psychological accessibility."

This is probably the most unique and important concept within the theory of crisis intervention. People in crisis are less defensive and more vulnerable to change than they are in non-crisis periods.

This heightened accessibility has obvious and very important implications when it comes to counseling a person in crisis. As Gerald Caplan has stated, "A relatively minor force, acting for a relatively short time, can switch the whole balance to one side or to the other—to the side of mental health or to the side of mental ill-health."* A crisis can be then a turning point in a person's emotional, mental, and spiritual health.

Halpern has verified this heightened psychological accessibility in his research on the defensiveness of people in crisis. He found that they tend to protect themselves less than other people and are more open for outside help and assistance toward change. This research validated Caplan's argument that people in crisis are more open to intervention of any kind.†

The period of heightened psychological accessibility generally peaks quickly and lasts for only a brief period of time. If the minister cannot establish a relationship quickly, or spends too much time gathering information, the person may move past the point of heightened accessibility, and greater amounts of time and effort will be required in counseling than would have been necessary during the time of crisis.

One way to explain this period of heightened psychological accessibility is to use Morley's diagram of crisis.‡ In diagram 2 the triangle represents an individual who is not

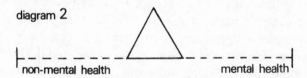

diagram 2

non-mental health   mental health

in crisis. This person is fairly stable; one of the sides of the triangle is firmly planted on a continuum between mental health and non-mental health. A large part of each of us is fairly stable and can be relied upon when we are not in crisis. We are less open to change. To lead normal lives we need a certain amount of such personality stability.

Diagram 3 illustrates a person who is in crisis, indicated

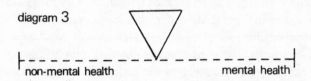

diagram 3

non-mental health   mental health

by the triangle which is tipped up on end. Here the person is in a state of "upsetness," or cognitive dissonance. Much less of the personality is firmly planted on the line between mental health and non-mental health. The individual wants to reestablish stability, and is therefore very susceptible to any influence from the inside or the outside which will aid in resolving the crisis. Thus with a minimal effort on the part of the minister, mental health professional, or family member, a maximum amount of leverage may be exerted upon the individual.

As I stated in *Suicide and Grief*, "during the period of crisis, with the individual's greater susceptibility to change, less counseling is required to aid him toward effective resolution of his problems. The difficulty frequently is that we do not help soon enough. When the crisis stage is past, it takes considerably more leverage to bring change because the 'triangle' is back on its base."* The brief period when the triangle is tipped up is so significant because of the emotional intensity, the cognitive dissonance, and the heightened vulnerability. Successful crisis intervention counseling makes maximum use of the heightened psychological accessibility of an individual in crisis.

10. The resolution of a crisis can be for better or for worse.

Although a person may experience considerable emotional pain during a crisis it can become a positive experience, a chance for growth. A person who lets a crisis go by without learning from it has wasted a valuable opportunity.

Most ministers have seen both adaptive and unadaptive reactions among the bereaved. I recall Agatha, a thirty-seven-year-old woman in Los Angeles who stated that, although she wished her husband had not died and she would not like to go through the grief again, she felt she was a better person, a more "alive" individual, as a result of the experience. Before the grief she was living in a rut, but since then she had increasingly valued her relationships with other people and with God. She still grieved, yet she felt emotionally stronger than she had in her whole life.

The opposite reaction is seen in fifty-seven-year-old Horace whom I counseled on a couple of occasions. For the ten years since his wife's death he had been going through life under a cloud. He was chronically depressed and exhausted, and had entered a mental hospital twice, totally out of touch with reality. In crisis, Horace had responded to the death of his wife in a most unadaptive way. Agatha, on the other hand, had successfully coped with the crises she had previously encountered.

11. A history of successful resolution of crises increases an individual's chances of successfully resolving each new crisis.

In the cases of Agatha and Horace, the vastly different reactions to bereavement were somewhat dependent upon how the two individuals had dealt with previous crises in their lives. Horace had a history of adapting poorly to stressful situations, especially the death of his mother.

12. Crises, besides causing upheaval in one's emotional, physical, and intellectual life, also cause a disturbance in one's values and sense of meaning in life. Every crisis has a religious potential. Crises raise basic questions such as:

What is the meaning of life? Is it worth the pain to continue living? Why did this happen to me? Why did God allow it?

The minister or counselor who deals with the emotional, physical, or intellectual and ignores the spiritual and "meaning" aspects of a person's crisis is not responding to the whole person or using his or her unique training. During crisis a person may be especially receptive to Christian values and meaning if they are sensitively portrayed by the minister.

Paul Tillich defined pastoral care as "helping encounter in the dimension of ultimate concern."* Upstanding members of a congregation may, during a crisis, question what they have previously affirmed in their Christian faith. In such a situation the minister must not be frightened, but remain emotionally "with" the person. His or her sensitivity and ministry of presence will help a person to weather these doubts.

13. Intervention in crises is not the exclusive domain of ministers and mental health professionals.

The empathy, warmth, and concern of nonprofessionals and "significant others" may be both necessary and sufficient in the resolution of a crisis. Therefore the crisis intervention counseling of the minister may frequently involve counseling to these other persons, enabling them to care more effectively for the person in crisis.

14. Every person comes into counseling with a certain set of expectations, the fulfillment of which is one of the most important factors in arriving at a positive outcome.

In some forms of traditional counseling the psychotherapist endeavors to go beneath the "presenting problem" and expectancies of the client to the "deeper" underlying problems. This may be valuable in traditional therapy; but in crisis intervention. wherever possible, it is most important for the minister to work toward the fulfillment of the individual's stated goals.

15. Situational aspects frequently are factors in sustain-

ing a crisis; the alteration of the situation (what some authors call environmental manipulation) can often change the course of a crisis positively.

Ruth Gorman, a twenty-nine-year-old Philadelphian whose husband had abandoned her five weeks before she sought counseling, was the mother of four children from two to eight years old. Ruth's crisis was precipitated when the utility companies turned off the electricity, gas, and telephone in the middle of the winter, and the landlord gave her two days to come up with the back rent or be put out in the street. She tried in vain for one whole day to borrow the money she needed. Finally she stumbled into a downtown church and told the minister her situation. Within the next twenty-four hours he was able to find her another apartment, arrange for several church members to help her move, and put her in touch with a social worker who would help her obtain money and food for herself and her children. The alteration of her environmental situation—moving to another apartment and receiving some money and food—resolved her crisis.

16. People in crisis often tend to pull away from the interpersonal relationships which they need just then more than at other times in their lives; positive interpersonal relationships can foster adaptive crisis resolution.

A significant factor in the resolution of Ruth's crisis was her willingness to seek help from others. Most authors writing about crisis theory emphasize that a person in crisis should not be viewed as an isolated individual but as an interacting member of a social system.

In crisis intervention the minister needs to realize that if, for instance, a man has just lost his job, the crisis may involve not just him but his wife and family as well. Persons in relationship need each other, and they need other caring people around them in a time of crisis.

People who are in the process of getting a divorce are frequently treated as "emotional lepers." Actually they need friends and relatives now more than at any other time in their lives, since they have lost what might have been their primary relationship. The lack of valuable interpersonal relationships can considerably heighten the distress of a person in crisis.

Equipped with a basic understanding of the dynamics and characteristics of crisis, ministers can begin to utilize these insights to relieve the distress of people coming to them for help. A model may be helpful at this point when it comes to putting theory into practice, and actually implementing crisis intervention in pastoral care and counseling.

3. A Design for Intervention

John Simon called his pastor at 11:45 Thursday evening. He and his wife had had another fight, and she wanted a divorce. Pastor Cole knew that John, twenty-nine, and Donna, twenty-seven, had been having trouble for the six years they had been married, though whenever he had visited them in their home they had always acted the "happily married couple." John did not want the divorce.

John asked Pastor Cole to come immediately but the pastor, determining that there was no immediate danger, set up an appointment for the next morning at his office. When they arrived Donna stated, "I came only because he wanted me to. I've made up my mind, I'm going to get a divorce and neither you nor anybody else can change my mind." She felt their relationship was beyond help.

John said the "problem" was that she wanted a divorce. Donna said John and everything he did was the "problem." Pastor Cole arranged to see the couple again four days later.

At the appointed hour John showed up alone. He said that Donna had forced him out of the house and he was staying at his brother's place. John cried through most of the session. All he could think about was the tremendous loss he had sustained, and all he wanted out of counseling was to get his wife back. "There is nothing left in life anymore without her," he said. "If she doesn't come back I'm going to kill myself."

How would you manage this situation? What would be the best approach in dealing with John Simon?

These questions deserve an immediate answer, as surely

as John needs immediate help. Perhaps we can wait to deal with them, however, until we have considered more fully a design for crisis intervention. The crisis intervention techniques which will be described in this chapter are designed to take full advantage of the healing and growth-fostering forces that already exist in individuals—especially those who in crisis may seem to be without them—and of the distinctive opportunities that inhere in the parish situation.

The Advantages of Crisis Counseling

Crisis intervention has several advantages over traditional counseling practice in times of a crisis such as that of John Simon. First, crisis intervention methods are designed specifically to deal with crises, not with other psychological problems. Just as there are certain methods which are especially effective with autistic children, or chronic depressive individuals, so crisis intervention techniques have been designed to take advantage of the unique aspects of a crisis.

Second, ministers sometimes encounter "backlash" from people with whom they have had long-term, in-depth counseling relationships. Because crisis intervention focuses on immediate problem solving, the parishioner need not fear that the minister will delve into all the nooks and crannies of his or her psyche, and there is less chance that the person, out of embarrassment, will resent the pastor or leave the church.

In the third place, crisis intervention is effective with individuals in low socioeconomic groups. Gerald F. Jacobson states, "Any successful approach to psychotherapy when the therapist and patient are psychosocial strangers must, at least at first, minimize the differences between the persons involved and maximize what unites them. . . . The more acute the crisis, the less the sense of strangeness, even with patients and therapists widely divergent in social background or age."* Especially among low socioeconomic groups a demand for immediate and concrete action rather than delaying gratification for the sake of long-term "mental health" goals, is common. Crisis intervention is geared to this need.

Fourth, crisis intervention techniques do not use up long periods of the pastor's time. Since a crisis' duration is at the most only four to six weeks, the minister will rarely enter into more than six counseling sessions.

Finally, crisis intervention is a method of counseling which can be practiced not only by ministers, but also by trained laypersons in the congregation. It is not necessary to have years and years of training in psychodynamics, pathology, or analysis to be an effective crisis intervener. On the other hand, it cannot be done effectively without some training and supervised practice.

Preparing to Counsel in Crisis

As ministers we need to be prepared to deal with crucial situations. The following are some "preparations" I have found valuable.

I constantly need to look at myself as a person, to be willing to accept the pain which leads to personal growth, to be aware that at times "I" get in the way of my counseling, and that at such times I need help. Help can take the form of consultation about the case with a minister or other mental health professional, or referral of the individual to another's care. (It is important to refer those persons whom I cannot help.) I need to know my own limitations in order to function effectively as a counselor.

I must continually learn to accept failure. Without getting into definitions of success and failure, I do know that sometimes, no matter how hard I try to rationalize, I feel as if I have failed. Sometimes I have indeed made some mistakes, but sometimes the people I seek to help fight off that help no matter how seriously they need it. There are individuals who would prefer to commit suicide rather than to share their deepest feelings with another person. For a person who experiences all change as loss, there will in crisis be mixed feelings about changing, and this may well affect the outcome of any attempt at intervention.

I also need to be sensitive to expectations others have of me as a pastor, the role they put me in as a result of their childhood experiences with a minister. Most people do not know how to act in counseling. Their impressions have been largely shaped by stereotypes. (I can still see the startled look on the face of a late-middle-aged woman who first saw a youngish-looking pastoral counselor without a tie or coat and exclaimed, "You're not *Doctor* Stone, are you? ! !") Another common stereotype is that ministers and counselors can wave a magic wand and solve any problem.

I need also to prepare for crisis intervention counseling by conditioning and improving my ability to cope with "negative" feelings—anger, sarcasm, and belittlement— directed toward me. In my freshman year in college I was canvassing for a local inner city church in Minneapolis. We were instructed to ask a few basic questions and then feel free to sit and talk with anyone who requested it. At one apartment I encountered a man in his forties who gruffly invited me in. After I had settled myself and asked five or six questions about his church affiliation he said, "You're religious—I have a question for you. My son was killed— run over by a car two weeks ago. Why did God do that? Why did God let that happen?" He proceeded to berate me about the hypocrisy of Christians, the foolishness of religion, and the fact that I had no answers to his questions. I ago- nized through his angry words and gesticulations—frozen to my chair with fear. If he had not been between me and the door I would have fled. After what seemed like hours but was probably twenty minutes, he broke down and cried, "You're the first one who has listened to me." Although I take no credit for the therapeutic way I handled the situa- tion—I listened because I couldn't think of a way out—I was able to give him the chance he needed to release his feelings about his son's death. Sometimes we have to wade through considerable negative emotions to be able to care for someone. I am not suggesting that we become emotional whipping posts. But you can expect at times to stay up late many evenings, miss your day off, and give of yourself extensively—only to receive no thanks—or even, as a fellow-pastor once described it, be "knifed in the back." In crises people will sometimes share things with you that they cannot later countenance having revealed.

I need to be aware of going into a crisis myself while doing crisis intervention. When this happens I lose my ability to relate in a calm and relaxed manner, and to see alternative solutions to the problem. Each counselor reacts to the anxiety of a crisis differently—one may talk too much, or not listen closely, or quote Scripture and send the person home, or give authoritarian dictates, or become paralyzed. Whatever your personal response to anxiety, you need to be sensitive to it, aware of it. The best way of coping when you sense yourself moving into a crisis is to share your burden with someone else—either by consulting with another pastor or mental health professional, inviting some other person to share your counseling responsibility (I strongly recommend this course whenever a parishioner is highly suicidal) or by referring the counselee to another source of help. The most valuable method for me has been to share the situation with at least one other person. I thus have a chance to release my own feelings and to see how someone else views the crisis.

A prerequisite basic for all pastoral care work is also necessary for crisis counseling—to genuinely care for the person in crisis. I sometimes find it easy to become so engrossed in my role, or techniques, or other responsibilities, that I lose sight of my basic mission to love others and see them as infinitely worthful persons. This aspect of preparation may seem so obvious that it need not be mentioned. Yet there are times when parishioners or counselees become

only "cases," problems, or new experiences rather than
people for whom Christ died.

The ABC Method of Crisis Intervention

The goal of crisis counseling is to assist persons in crisis
to regain at least their prior level of functioning, and hopefully to grow to even higher levels. The first task is to determine if a crisis really exists. Switzer believes this can be
done by answering three questions: "(1) Has there been a
recent (within a few weeks) onset of the troublesome feelings and/or behavior? (2) Have they tended to grow pro-
gressively worse? (3) Can the time of the onset be linked
with some external event, some change in the person's life
situation?"* If you can say yes to all three questions, a
crisis most likely exists.

The model of crisis intervention offered here is my adap-
tation of the "ABC" method which was first formulated by
Warren L. Jones, a Los Angeles psychiatrist, as a technique
of counseling for treating crises.† (His method was further
developed and confirmed by Howard J. Clinebell, Jr. and
David K. Switzer as well as such theorists as Carkhuff, Ivey,
and Glasser.‡)

In the ABC method of counseling there are three components: (A) *A*chieve contact with the person; (B) *B*oil
down the problem to its essentials; and (C) *C*ope actively
with the problem. It should be noted at the beginning that
this method does not necessarily imply a progression from
A to *B* to *C*; two or three steps can and frequently do occur
at the same time. For example, although you may already
be boiling down the problem from the very onset of counseling, the most important thing going on even at that time
is the achieving of contact, the establishing of a relationship.

A. Achieving contact with the person in crisis

The initial step for counseling an individual in crisis is
to achieve contact, or establish a therapeutic relationship.

Psychotherapists traditionally refer to the end in view here as rapport. The relationship in question may already be there, if the minister has previously seen the people through normal developmental crises; and if it is, this can speed the initial phase of crisis intervention. The relationship not only serves to relax the parishioners but also becomes the means through which the minister can later move them from catharsis—the release of emotions—to a point of action. The counseling relationship is not the end-all of counseling, but the basis upon which the minister builds the counseling process toward the goal of changed behavior.

A relationship of trust and empathy is no less important in crisis intervention than in any other form of counseling or pastoral care. However, since persons in crisis are less defensive, it will generally—though not always—take less time and effort to establish the relationship.

The minister needs to have developed some basic relation-building skills. These can be distinguished as attending behaviors and listening.

Attending behaviors

Attending behaviors are those physical acts of the minister which help to produce a relaxed and comfortable environment for the parishioner and communicate the interest and concern of the counselor. They are a physical way of saying "I care and am concerned about you." A variety of behaviors may be mentioned in this connection.

One attending behavior important to the development of rapport is symbolic nourishing. Perhaps the earliest way any of us experienced the care and concern of another was through the nursing we received at our mother's breast. Offering a coffee cake to a bereaved family is an example of symbolic nourishing behavior. We can show our concern to someone in crisis by allowing that person to sit in a comfortable, relaxed environment and have a cup of coffee or a glass of water.

The posture we take communicates our interest and readiness to respond. The most helpful posture is that of facing the client and leaning forward slightly in that direction. This closes the physical distance and also indicates interest. Think about it for a moment: when you are deeply interested in what someone is saying, you often move to the edge of your chair to listen.

Another way we experience care and concern from earliest infancy is through having our parents hold and cuddle us. The need for care and stroking does not stop in infancy but continues throughout life. One way to "hold" clients, which will usually meet their needs without frightening them, is to take their hands in yours or put your arm around their shoulders when they are crying or expressing deep pain.

Looking into the eyes of the parishioner is one of the most powerful attending behaviors for communicating concern. Some people cannot verbalize without this eye contact. When I was talking one day with one of my professors in graduate school, he turned around to wipe off the blackboard; as he did so I stopped talking without even noticing it. He turned and said to me, "You need eye contact, don't you?" The amount of eye contact required depends on the needs of the individual. If you are giving too much, he or she will let you know either verbally or by looking away or pulling back in the chair. If you are not giving enough eye contact people will tend to share their problems and feelings more slowly or superficially.

The room in which you receive a parishioner needs to communicate calmness, confidentiality, and openness. It is best not to counsel a person across a desk. People in a counseling situation should sit on comfortable chairs of roughly equal height, facing each other. Parishioners need to feel that what they say is totally confidential and will not be heard outside the room.

The second important skill in establishing a relationship is that of listening, which in some respects can be considered an attending behavior. If you give your full and undivided attention to what the persons in crisis are saying, and encourage them to tell their story, you communicate your caring and concern through the way you hear what they say. Effective listening is really invaluable for crisis intervention. The following are some suggestions for effective listening.

It is important not to allow yourself to be distracted by outside noises, interruptions, and phone calls, or by inner distractions such as thinking about all the things you have to do that day. Your parishioners will generally be aware if you are distracted, and as a result will not reveal as much about themselves.

Vary your attending behavior to make it congruent with what the client is expressing. If Pastor Good is thinking about a funny joke he heard at lunch and a slight smile breaks out on his face just as his parishioner is talking about something very sad, the parishioner will know that the pastor is not listening. We need to feel free to cry with people who are communicating something sad, and to laugh and rejoice with them when they are talking about something joyful.

It is also necessary to have a purpose for listening. Know what you are listening for. You will be looking especially for the "presenting problem" and the precipitator of the crisis. You will want to know how the persons perceive the emotionally hazardous situation and what methods of coping and what resources they have tried thus far in dealing with the crisis. You will also begin to listen for how they are experiencing the stress of the crisis—so that when you get to *B*, the boiling down process, you can help them focus on what the crisis means to them.

It is important, especially in the early phases of developing a relationship, to be nonjudgmental; that is, to suspend your judgment and allow the person in crisis to release his or her feelings. In this connection it can often be more important to listen than to speak. If we immediately judge what people have done as "wrong," we are not apt to understand their reasons, or the pain they feel as a result.

As part of achieving contact it is valuable to allow the person in crisis to release his or her feelings. An important aspect of the listening process, however, does involve speaking—communicating to the persons that we do hear them, that we are listening, by mirroring back to them the feelings we have heard them express. This can be done by making statements such as: "You must have felt very angry," "You seem very sad," "I feel you are confused as to what to do"; or, "What I hear you saying is . . ." and here rephrasing but not adding to or deleting from the basic feeling being communicated.

Individuals in crisis sometimes have difficulty saying clearly what they want to express, and in such instances the counselor needs to be patient. It is valuable in the first interview to allow for long pauses before responding to what the persons have said. In their confusion, their mental processes are not functioning as they otherwise would, and they may be struggling to verbalize a pain which is so deep that they have difficulty putting it into words. How, for example, can you express in words the depth of pain you experience immediately after the death of someone close to you?

As you listen to the person in crisis, you will soon discern important common themes. They will come out either by being stated with great intensity, or by being repeated over and over again (just as a good speaker reiterates his main points in different ways). These common themes will be valuable in helping the clients to focus on the essence of their distress.

Another important part of listening is to narrow the focus

of the communication. In crisis intervention, unlike some methods of psychotherapy, it soon becomes important to let the clients know that time is of the essence. The minister, once he is confident that it will not be anxiety-producing, begins to communicate the impression that they "don't have all day" by selectively reinforcing those subjects which are related to the crisis and by withholding response to those which are irrelevant. I think it is best to allow considerable freedom in the first one-third to one-half of the first interview, but thereafter to focus the conversation on the actual crisis. Often all the minister needs to say is, "That sounds like something important that we need to deal with, but I don't think it's directly related to your present problem. As soon as we have resolved this crisis we can spend more time talking about that." Otherwise without realizing it, the minister may encourage a return to ineffective childhood behaviors: by allowing rambling or unfocused conversation or talk which focuses mainly on past events; by not calling upon clients to use their own resources of self-observation, self-restraint, and self-responsibility; by allowing them to seek detachment from their feelings without being called back by the comments of the counselor; or by permitting anything to keep the clients from focusing on the immediate crisis.

I believe it is important for you as a counselor in the midst of a crisis to be empathetic, calm and stable, active and intrusive. You can often communicate hope through the very confidence you have in your own capacities to understand and help. Through the establishment of a relationship, especially through attending behaviors and skillful listening, the minister shows active concern for the client. You also thereby communicate intensity, responding to the person's strong feelings at a comparable level of strength.

Most counselors and psychotherapists are trained to avoid taking too much responsibility in counseling. In crisis counseling this may sometimes be ill-advised. The crisis counselor needs to take responsibility by being active and assertive (even breaking confidentiality if necessary) in order to make decisions for the person who cannot handle the decision-making process in his or her own self-interest. The person needs a counselor who does more than reflect feelings or offer passive support. In other words, it is the counselor's task to take responsibility, but only to the extent needed. As Thomas N. Rusk puts it, "Do for others that which they cannot do for themselves, and no more."*

B. Boiling down the problem to its essentials

The second step of the ABC method of crisis intervention involves boiling down the problem. This requires responding to and focusing on the feelings and meanings of the clients, so that they can define in their own minds what has happened, what they are actually feeling, and why. The boiling down phase calls upon the counselor's skills of responding and focusing.

Responding

Responding is one of the basic dimensions of all human interchange; communication, verbal or nonverbal, is not complete until there is response. The minister has already begun responding to the person in crisis while achieving contact (A) but during the (B) phase the pastor will have fewer and shorter periods of mere listening. The response of the minister will be in three areas: nonverbal behavior, feelings, and meaning.

You as a minister need to be aware, first of all, of your clients' nonverbal physical behavior. It will give you clues to their experience and feelings. Special attention is devoted to their physical energy and activity. An individual with a low energy level will find it difficult to cope actively with the problem (C). Energy level is reflected in physical activity; children are good examples of persons who are usually "alive." People in crisis, unlike the healthy child, tend to function with low levels of physical energy because their pressures and conflicts have immobilized them and drained off their energy. The lower the physical activity, the more direct and active a counseling response will be required from the minister.

You need also to be aware of incongruent behavior, discrepancies between what people say and what they do. A man in a counseling session said he wasn't upset about his daughter's pregnancy, but his red neck and white knuckles suggested that he was not facing up to his true feelings; he could not admit to experiencing a crisis. The alert minister responded to the clues by pointing them out to the father and asking him what he was really feeling.

People in crisis will usually express those feelings which dominate them. The minister will be of great assistance if he can help them identify and articulate those dominant feelings. Sometimes feelings are verbally expressed. But even when they are not, it is to the client's feelings that the minister responds. You pay close attention to the tone of voice, facial expressions, posture, and hand gestures, but feelings is what you look for. One of the best ways to determine how a person in crisis feels is to ask yourself how you would feel if you were that person. It is valuable to have role-played a number of typical crises, and reflected on some of the crises you have experienced yourself, so that you will recognize in your clients' presentation and behavior clues to what they are feeling.

As in achieving contact, so in the boiling down process it is good to suspend judgment. It is also valuable at least to try—however difficult—to suspend your entire frame of reference, i.e., to hold in abeyance those attitudes (racial, religious, social, economic, political) which would prevent you from entering into your client's world of feeling. In doing so you communicate respect for the person's own frame of reference.

Once you have determined, whether from words or actions, how a person really feels, it is important to communicate your understanding of these feelings. As counselors we seek to assure that we have responded accurately to people's feelings by trying to articulate them in the way they themselves might do, in an "interchangeable" way. A response is said to be interchangeable if the minister expresses the same feelings as the parishioner has communicated—no more and no less. The "You feel . . ." formula provides one way to do this: "You feel sad," "You feel angry," "You feel upset."

It is good to build your skill in responding to feelings by broadening your own feeling vocabulary. You can practice such responses by listing fifty alternative words and expressions for each of the following dominant feelings: sadness, happiness, anger. Try this for a few minutes now, allowing yourself to use slang, colloquialisms, figures of speech, anything to accomplish the purpose.

Ultimately the concern in responding has to do with the significance of the crisis for the person experiencing it— and of the feelings for the person expressing them. Meaning can be understood only where there is an understanding of both the feeling and the content expressed by the person in crisis. The same feelings are common to us all, but the specific content of the feelings is different for each individual. The feeling is "happy"; the content may be "for being promoted to assistant manager." The feeling is "angry"; the content may be "toward my husband who won't let me have sex." Content clarifies feelings and together they offer meaning. A simple way to express this is given in the equation: Feeling ("You feel . . .") plus content ("because . . .") = meaning. This meaning is discerned not only through "You feel depressed" but through "You feel depressed because you lost your job").

In step *B* of the ABC method it is vitally important that you not just respond to the feeling, but that you determine the content of the feeling so that the meaning of the crisis can be distilled out.

Focusing

Individuals are frequently unaware or not fully aware of the precipitating stress and its consequences. The focusing process aims at prompt identification of the nature of the threat, with clarification of the relevant circumstances and conflicts. Such identification and clarification can help to resolve the crisis. Important in the boiling down step is this focusing on the present situation and on the source of the stress. If the crisis can be defined clearly, and the nature of the threat to the person clarified, a plan for its solution can often be created; indeed, it may emerge spontaneously out of the individual's own thinking.

Since many who are in crisis are avoiding reality and defending themselves against pain, a part of the counselor's task is to help them face up to it. The minister creates an environment in which the person feels comfortable enough to face up to the crisis and the event that precipitated it. In focusing, the minister needs to be aware of: (1) the precipitating event; (2) the threat to (possibly loss of) a relationship or social role perceived by the person as significant; (3) the individual's coping methods and resources; and (4) new factors or conditions which may invalidate his or her traditional methods of coping.

Focusing includes filtering out irrelevant data. Persons in crisis sometimes share material which is meaningless to the situation but which they do not know is meaningless. If seemingly unrelated material is brought up, the minister can try to relate it to the present crisis—or show its irrelevance —with a statement such as, "I wonder how you see this relating to your immediate problem."

The ABC method does not utilize traditional diagnostic tools such as extensive history-taking or psychological testing. Anything resembling such assessment is done only to identify and explain the crisis, for the outcome of a crisis is seldom determined to any great extent by factors which came before the crisis itself. Only those past experiences which remain with the client as currently significant factors are relevant.

Once the situation is accurately assessed, the minister portrays this assessment to the person as simply and directly as possible, communicating the essence of the dilemma. This communication has been called "consensual formulation." Minister and parishioner mutually formulate an understanding of what has happened, and put it into words. Only then is the distressed person able to move into later phases of the process, examine various alternative methods of dealing with the present crisis, choose the alternatives which seem appropriate, and mobilize the available resources. The minister and the client may not always be able to develop consensual formulation, but if it is not developed there is less chance for growth to occur through the counseling, even if the crisis is resolved adaptively.

Focusing on the problem's components accomplishes a basic purpose of crisis counseling, namely, to help the person pull out of the tailspin. The development of a consensual formulation can in itself reduce the anxiety level and enhance self-esteem for the person in crisis.

C. Coping actively with the problem

In the final stage of the ABC method the minister helps people in crisis to evaluate and mobilize their resources, develop a plan of action, and make specific changes directed toward resolving the crisis. One of the worst things a person in crisis can do is to become isolated. Isolation often leads to bouts of depression and self-pity. The pastor needs to help persons examine what alternative courses of action can be taken to reshape their lives, and then challenge them to act upon one or more of these alternatives. That help usually comprises five components: establishment of goals; inventory of resources; formulation of alternatives; action; and review and refinement.

Establishment of goals

Ideally, at this point in the ABC method the minister has established a relationship, allowed catharsis and expression of negative feelings, and helped the persons to boil down and specifically define and understand the crisis. The next task is to help them establish goals. This is usually a fairly simple task inasmuch as crisis counseling aims only at the removal of symptoms and the achievement of a level of functioning as high as or higher than before.

The goal determines the direction in which the counseling will proceed and toward which the courses of action will be aimed. It is always best to be as specific as possible in defining goals, and to define them in observable terms so that their achievement is measurable. It is far more helpful to establish small and short-term aims, and attain them, than to set up lofty, long-term goals which cannot be reached and will only bring disappointment.

Inventory of resources

After the goal has been delineated, you will need to help the persons take inventory of their internal and external resources. People in crisis frequently have trouble rationally reviewing their resources. The minister may therefore have to take the lead.

Internal resources are those methods of coping which all of us have within us, upon which we can draw in the face of the problems we encounter each day. Sometimes the counselees may not be aware of having these resources. They need to be pointed out to them. (e.g., "You say you can't tell people what you feel, but I see you doing a great job of telling your feelings to me.") One significant internal resource is the history of handling past crises. The minister who has gone through developmental or past situational crises with the parishioners can point out what led to their successful resolution.

External resources include such things as friends, family, church, spiritual resources, community groups, and finances. People who are in crisis very often pull away from meaningful interpersonal involvement and feel totally alone. A relatively modest amount of need-fulfillment on the part of other people is often enough to exert a great deal of positive influence on the crisis. The support and gratification which was offered in the past by a now-lost relationship may be achieved through a new significant other person, or the strengthening of an already existing relationship.

Individuals who are emotionally close to a person in crisis frequently need pastoral care themselves. They are under greater than normal pressures during the counselee's crisis, and may themselves need special guidance and support. It is good for the minister to have available a group of people in the congregation who are capable and willing to move into crisis situations and are not frightened by them. The persons in crisis can also be drawn into ongoing fellowship or prayer groups within the church where they will find additional support. The worship function of the church can also be an important resource in a crisis, for example, a funeral service, or confession, or an order for the blessing of a civil marriage.

Community resources may be available to those in crisis. If they have recently been in counseling, it is good to send them back to the same counselor. If they say "Oh, he didn't help me" this should be carefully evaluated before being accepted at face value. Persons in crisis may resist listing as resources people whom they feel are unwilling or unable to help. It is true that these people often become irritated by the chronic whining, depression, and helplessness of the person in crisis, but in my experience they could become mobilized if they were made aware of both the person's need and how they could in fact help. One task in crisis intervention, then, is to help these significant others to care for the troubled person as effectively as possible.

Formulation of alternatives

Once the counselees have developed goals and reviewed their resources, the minister and the parishioners "brainstorm" alternative ways of action which might facilitate these goals. The persons in crisis are encouraged to develop their own alternatives. Both "good" and "bad" ideas are included on the list; for example, when dealing with a suicidal individual I include committing suicide as one of the options.

The minister can then jar the parishioners' thinking by suggesting other possible courses of action. This is not a matter of advice-giving but an attempt to broaden the horizons of persons who may still be "cognitively constricted" and honestly cannot think of alternatives. In almost all cases, however, the individual chooses personally the course of action to be actually taken.

From the list of alternatives all of the relevant and workable courses of action should next be selected. For example, the single mother who feels pressured by the responsibilities of the home, three children, and a full-time job may not be able to quit her job and stay home. If she has no other means of income, such a course would be impossible even if desirable. The parishioner needs to evaluate with the minister the various courses of action that seem open. The task is to weigh these options against one's personal values (money, free time, good job, family). If people find that a certain alternative will go against most of their values, that alternative can be eliminated. For the man who is having financial problems, but values very much his work in the church, his free time, and his family, twenty hours a week of "moonlighting" on a second job will violate almost all of his values.

After courses of action have been weighed in terms of values, their potential effectiveness is considered. The minister and client try to estimate whether the alternatives under review will effectively lead to the chosen goals. After the client finishes evaluating the potential effectiveness of the alternatives, the minister can step in as an "expert" and share information about them from his or her own experience, or from the experiences of other counselees (always maintaining confidentiality of course). For example, to a recently divorced man who was isolating himself and yet wanted to meet people I said, "I have known several people who found the single-adults group at our neighboring church helpful after their divorces."

It is very important that, after reviewing the various courses of action, the persons in crisis choose one or possibly two to embark upon. This sometimes requires gentle urging on the part of the minister. I frequently find it valuable to write down the commitment on a piece of paper for myself, and have the counselees write it down as well. Here they make a "covenant" to begin to do the chosen alternatives before the next counseling visit. They are now taking small, concrete steps toward achieving their goal. At this point of decision and covenant commitment individuals who want counseling only to express emotions and "go home feeling better" will usually quit. If a client does not want to choose, the minister can either urge the person to do so, or go back several steps in the process and evaluate the resistance. Sometimes an abrasive attitude on the part of the counselor will irritate a person into action; but this tool must be used with considerable caution and, if successful, should be immediately replaced by an attitude of understanding and empathetic participation.

Action

After the commitment, action must follow. This step is very important because it helps reverse any tendency the client may have had toward dependence upon the counselor. It is important that persons begin implementing their chosen alternatives. Action counters the paralysis involved in the crisis, and encourages people to do something about their problems whether they feel like it or not. As O. Hobart Mowrer states, "It is easier to act your way into a new way of feeling than to feel your way into a new way of action."* Or, in Clinebell's words, "The person's personality or self is like a muscle. When you use a muscle it grows stronger . . . if you don't use the muscle, the muscle begins to atrophy and waste away."† The resumption of personal control sometimes comes slowly but is accomplished in time.

Infinite patience is necessary on the part of the counselor. Sometimes there is resistance at this crucial stage and clients will "forget" or "not have time" to begin acting on their chosen alternatives. Sometimes I sense that they are trying to make me angry so they can justify breaking off the counseling and have "righteous" reasons for their leave (escape). Resistance needs to be aired immediately and dealt with. The client should not be allowed to slide without being confronted. I repeatedly remind clients of their freedom of choice to do or not to do what will help them with their problems, and that I will aid them in any way I can to achieve their goals but (except in extreme emergencies) will not do it for them. Sometimes the clients' anxiety will make action difficult, but there are ways in which an anxiety-laden individual can be approached that may reduce the anxiety and thus the risk of failure. Most valuable for me in this connection have been role playing, the sharing of personal problems in a small group, and the mapping out of small successive steps to achieve the goal.

Review and refinement

In many ways review and refinement is not a separate part but an ongoing function in all counseling. The client and the counselor must continually evaluate whether the new behavior is effective toward reaching the goal of crisis resolution. They also need to examine whether the chosen goal is still what the person wants, and if it is not, to alter it.

I knew a family in which the mother was frequently in

and out of mental hospitals. Their first tactic to support her in getting well was to do whatever she wanted. When she did not improve, however, and the family became more chaotic, they decided to act in such a way that her paranoia would not disrupt the rest of the family unit. The father and two children were able to develop a strong bond, and the family learned that it could function whether the mother was at home with them or in the hospital. Ultimately they did not exclude her, but they would no longer let her dominate and disintegrate the family.

In the final sessions of crisis counseling it is always valuable for the pastoral counselor to reiterate the learning which has taken place, and directly encourage the persons to use their new-found strengths and coping skills for solving the future problems and crises which are certain to occur.

Follow-Up of the Counseling Process

Follow-up with the person or family in crisis is valuable for several reasons. It deepens your relationship with them and reaffirms your caring. It determines if they are continuing to do what is needed to help with their crisis. It communicates that they have a continuing responsibility to do something specific about their problems and not just to express feelings. Following up does not mean "checking up," but expressing your interest in their continued well-being. It offers an additional chance for expression of emotions and assessing the new behavior. Sharing recent feelings and further evaluating the courses of action naturally leads to further new learning.

Follow-up also offers the minister a chance to deal with the residue of a crisis. Besides leftover feelings of hurt or anger, there is sometimes a gnawing anxiety that "it will happen again." There may even be some other, perhaps more basic problem for which the person needs to seek long-term help. A successful salesman while putting up a TV antenna on his house fell off the roof and broke his

back. The injury in itself caused a crisis, but as they dealt
with the problem, it soon became apparent to both himself
and his wife that they had some even more serious marital
problems. After resolving the initial crisis surrounding the
injury, the couple began marriage counseling.

Follow-up does not necessarily take place in the minister's office. A lunch date, a phone call, a stop at someone's
shop, or a friendly visit in the home all provide the occasion
for seeing if the crisis has been adequately resolved.

Having traced some helpful methods of crisis counseling
from *A* to *C*, including the matter of follow-up, let us now
go back to John and Donna Simon where we left them at
the beginning of the chapter. Donna was firm about wanting the divorce and refused marriage counseling. It was
evident to the pastor that John was in considerable stress.
Using Switzer's three criteria for establishing the existence
of a crisis, Pastor Cole found:

(1) A recent onset of bad feelings—after six years of
marriage, feelings had become overstrained as of last Thursday night; (2) The feelings growing steadily worse—they
continued to intensify to the point where Donna had forced
John out of the house and started divorce proceedings, and
John was now thinking of killing himself; (3) An external
event triggering the recent surge of feeling—there had been
trouble in the marriage before but it reached a new level of
intensity with the Thursday night fight, when John called
the pastor.

Certain that a crisis was present, Pastor Cole began to
apply the ABC method of crisis intervention. Three major
steps were involved in the actual handling of the situation.

1. *A*chieve contact. Pastor Cole already had a relationship with John; he had seen him in church regularly. The
pastor was not rejecting or judgmental, though John feared
he might be. If John had not had a prior relationship of
trust with his minister, he probably would not have sought
counsel from anyone.

The pastor practiced most of the attending behaviors. He faced John, leaned toward him, and maintained eye contact. John responded to the attending behaviors and active listening, and in the second session broke down and sobbed. He felt totally without hope. He was "cognitively constricted" and could see no other alternatives than either forcing Donna to live with him, or committing suicide. The pastor allowed John to tell him the full story, to lean upon him and draw strength from him.

2. *B*oil down. Focusing the problem was somewhat difficult for the pastor in the second counseling session. John cried a great deal. He kept repeating: "If she doesn't come back I'm going to kill myself." "I want my wife back—that's all I want." It was a long time before any two-way communication could develop. The pastor allowed considerable release of feelings but finally urged that they focus on what John could realistically do.

Another difficulty was rooted in Pastor Cole's assumption that, since divorce was the precipitating event, it was also the heart of the crisis. With continued listening, however, he was able to boil down the crisis to its central meaning for John: "John, if I'm hearing you right, Donna's divorcing you has left you feeling a strong loss and very lonely. You don't feel very much like a man." John responded, "Yeah, I feel like I've lost my manhood—it's terrible." In these brief summations John and the pastor developed a "consensual formulation" of the essence of the crisis. They stated it as it was most sharply experienced. The crisis of John's loss and loneliness had caused a severe identity struggle within him. John relaxed somewhat (and so did Pastor Cole) after they felt they had articulated the crisis at its sharpest point. Sometimes just the process of developing a consensual formulation is all that is needed to turn a crisis around.

In John's case, however, the pastor knew that he also had to challenge John to act, to cope constructively through concrete action. Before doing this, however, he needed to assess accurately John's threats: "You are thinking of suicide? How do you plan on doing it? Do you own a gun? Do you have bullets? Is the gun loaded? Where is it?"* Pastor Cole found that John did in fact have a gun, and the ammunition with which to kill himself; the previous night he had even loaded it and was playing with it. John had definitely decided how he would commit suicide, and he had the external means and the inner stress necessary to carry it out. This was a clear indication that John's suicide lethality was high, and that the pastor would need to respond actively.

3. *C*ope actively. John's only goal was to get his wife back. The pastor suggested that this goal didn't appear likely, but that he would work with John on it and help him consider alternative ways of achieving it. The pastor inventoried John's resources, internal and external, and concluded that he didn't have many. John had not faced any severe crises in the past; he had few friends; he didn't like his job, and was afraid they might fire him if he continued complaining about his problems; he was a dependent person who had never shaped his own identity. Pastor Cole summarized John's three main resources: his work (though he didn't like his job, he did like the type of work he was doing); his brother and sister-in-law; and the pastor.

Because of John's limited resources, relatively high suicide lethality, and strong dependency, the pastor decided to end the second session by helping him write a calendar of all the things he would do in the next four days before they met again. He tried to insure that John would be active and involved with people on each of those days. John committed himself to live by that calendar. He further promised that he would call Pastor Cole at any time, day or night, if he felt he was going to commit suicide.

At the next session, John and the pastor discussed ways of reaching the goal of getting Donna to come back. John decided that since he "wasn't much of a man" he would try to be more independent and autonomous rather than "acting like a baby like I am now." He chose several strategies to accomplish this and committed himself to them. He soon started involving himself with people, making new friends, joining a community group, and acting more mature among his business associates. The pastor confronted him at once whenever John appeared to become overly dependent on him, or on others.

John committed himself to several alternatives and he acted on them. He didn't do all this in a week but within the space of three or four weeks. When he came back to the pastor and said he couldn't do a couple of the things to which he had committed himself, the pastor reflected, "It appears that you want to be led by the hand when we both know you *can* do them and do them yourself." Here the pastor was somewhat abrasive but he felt now that the relationship could tolerate it. John at first became angry, but then admitted that he too knew he could do it but was afraid. They talked about this fear and did some role playing.

Soon after implementing his courses of action John began to change his goal. As he worked through the initial weeks of grief the former goal of "getting her back" evolved into the new goal of "being my own man"—being a more mature adult who, though deeply hurt by the loss of his wife, wanted to become a better and more self-actualizing person.

After six sessions (about four weeks) John lost his job. Instead of crying over the layoff and threatening suicide, as he had done in his earlier loss, he made up resumés and flew to a convention in Chicago where he actually received a dozen job offers. This was gratifying and helped him to realize that he was a competent adult.

After the crisis was resolved, the pastor referred John to a counseling group. In the company of other growing persons he continued to develop his skills in interpersonal relationships—and an identity of his own.

Referral

Sometimes the best treatment we can offer individuals in crisis is to direct them to others who specialize in the types of service which will best meet their needs. "Properly conceived, referral is a means of using a team effort to help a troubled person. . . . It employs the division-of-labor principle that is the basis of interprofessional cooperation."*

There are two types of referral. In the first, the major responsibility is given over to another professional. This is frequently necessary when the person in crisis is psychotic, seriously suicidal or homicidal, or needs hospitalization. The second form of referral, more common to the minister in crisis counseling, involves retaining major responsibility for the person's care but sending the individual to a specialist for specific types of help, perhaps to a family debt counselor for assistance with financial planning.

Referral of your parishioner to an outside source is not a sign of failure. Often it is inevitable. Assuming you are a good pastoral counselor, that you are a healer, a guide, a reconciler, and a sustainer, it is nevertheless important— and the mark of a good counselor—that you know when to refer. The question is actually a matter of timing, taking into consideration both the condition of the parishioner and your own limitations. Time, skill, and emotional objectivity all play a role in determining when it is best to refer a parishioner to more specialized care.

Assuming that you have the expertise to deal with a particular person's crisis, it is important to determine whether or not you also have the time to handle the situation adequately. You need to ask yourself quite frankly: Will my other responsibilities be seriously neglected because of the time I give to this individual? Can I really limit the person to only so many minutes or so many sessions per week? Can I honestly and firmly restrict my telephone availability? Such limitations sometimes involve a cost to the counselee.

Assuming that you have the time, in some crisis situations it may be that your skill and experience will be far less helpful to the individual than that of a counselor who has some highly developed skill and experience in dealing with a particular problem. A good illustration is heroin addiction; few counselors and ministers, unless actually involved in a drug treatment center, are equipped to treat it effectively.

Some questions you might ask yourself in determining if you have the necessary skills to handle a particular crisis are: Do I feel comfortable working with this person? Can I be sure I am not misinterpreting this person's situation? After perhaps three or four sessions, is the person showing growth? Am I fostering negative dependency? As a rule of thumb, it is important to refer immediately to a mental health professional any person who is or appears to be psychotic, violent, seriously suicidal, homicidal, or whose behavior is noticeably bizarre.

Finally, the minister possessing both time and skill needs to avoid "hooking in" to the counseling situation his or her own feelings of threat, anxiety, fear, or insecurity. Some danger signals to watch for: When my own feelings get in the way of my ability to help the client; when a problem is raised which I have never resolved in my own life; when I have overburdened myself and have too little to offer in terms of time and caring; and when the approval of the individual counselee becomes so important to me that I feel my own status is at stake in the situation. In short, the key to successfully referring people, as to effective functioning in every phase of crisis intervention, may lie in whether or not I am able to act creatively, on the basis of my own limitations, with respect to my own emotional security, stability, and objectivity at the time.

4. Portraits in Crisis

Crises are not all alike. Caplan, Mason, and Kaplan, researchers in the field of crisis theory, believe that crises differ in two ways: according to whether they are developmental or situational; and according to the type of challenge or hazard involved, such as death of a loved one or significant personal injury. They found that, despite the diversity, "in any subcategory of crises, there appear to be certain regularly occurring psychological . . . tasks" which appear repeatedly.* Although the precipitators of crises can be as varied as the people who experience them, there are at the core of every crisis some basic dynamics which can be observed. If this were not the case we would not be able to study crisis intervention in general, but could only study the dynamics and treatment of specific crises.

This chapter will explore several different cases of people in crisis and how their pastors used the ABC method of crisis intervention with them. It is suggested that the reader project himself or herself into the situation and not only think about how to counsel the person in each case—for there is no one best way—but also try to define the precipitator of the crisis, the individual's perception of it, and, with the details presented, a "consensual formulation" for the person.

A Case of Attempted Suicide

Background

Pastor Anderson was exhausted from all the activities of a usual Sunday—two services, a special church council meeting in the afternoon, and the youth group that evening. It was close to midnight when he had gone to bed. Within minutes, just as he had begun to slide into that delightful phase halfway between waking and sleeping, the telephone rang.

The caller, Rick Patton, age forty-seven, was phoning about his forty-five-year-old wife, Rebecca. They had been married over twenty years and had no children. Pastor Anderson had never met or talked with the couple before.

The immediate situation

The speech at the other end of the line was excited and rapid. Rick blurted, "My wife has taken a lot of pills . . . I don't know what to do." The crisis precipitator for Rick was the threatened (and potentially real) loss of the most significant relationship in his life. He perceived this as very disastrous. His coping methods were temporarily paralyzed. He had done nothing for the first five minutes; then he thought of calling Pastor Anderson, whose name had been given to him four weeks before when the couple moved from Wisconsin to Florida.

Intervention

Before Pastor Anderson was able to intervene he had to deal with his own feelings. The adrenalin flowed through his body, and he found himself asking mainly informational questions of Rick. For the first minute or two the pastor too was paralyzed; he had read what to do in a suicide situation and he had previously counseled several people who had threatened suicide, but this was his first experience with someone who had actually done something destructive to herself.

Just as Pastor Anderson's anxiety had begun to ease a bit and he felt somewhat better able to cope with the situation, the caller thrust the phone into his wife's hand. So far Pastor Anderson had learned who the caller was (name and address) and what he was calling about. He had asked what the drug was (Secanol) and how many were taken (remainder of bottle—number unknown), and when (five or ten minutes previously).

But when Rebecca Patton took the phone she was able only to mumble incoherently. Pastor Anderson could not understand what she was saying. He tried yelling into the phone to arouse her. Then he heard a thud and the clang of the receiver as it hit the floor. She had evidently collapsed into unconsciousness.

Pastor Anderson had been on the phone now for four or five minutes. There had been little time for developing a relationship. He realized that he had to take a directive role. When Rick came back to the phone screaming that his wife had passed out, Anderson said, "OK. Here is what we are going to do." The pastor could not wait for Rick to mobilize his coping abilities; he gently but firmly gave orders.

Pastor Anderson first told Rick to leave their phone connection open, go to a neighbor's house, and phone the fire department, then tell the neighbor what had happened and enlist help. Rick balked at this suggestion, saying he had only been in town four weeks and did not know his neighbors. Pastor Anderson responded, "Listen, when your wife's life is in danger you don't worry about things like that. People are usually willing to help in a time of crisis."

After five minutes that seemed like an eternity Rick returned to the phone. He had made the call and had enlisted the help of the man who lived next door to him, a police car was pulling up in front, and he had to hang up. Pastor Anderson requested that Rick call him from the hospital.

At 1:30 A.M. Pastor Anderson's phone rang again. Rick said the ambulance had arrived very quickly, his wife's stomach was pumped, and the doctor said she was going to be all right. Pastor Anderson suggested that she see a counselor. Rick said she had already made an appointment to see a psychologist, but that was still two weeks away.

Anderson let him know that most counselors will see a person sooner if a crisis exists, and he strongly recommended that Rick call the psychologist first thing in the morning. Rick agreed to do so.

Follow-up

Early Monday afternoon Pastor Anderson called Rick. He learned that Rebecca was already out of the hospital and was seeing the psychologist that very afternoon. Pastor Anderson told Rick to call him if he could be of any further help. The following week, he stopped at their home to see if he could relate Rick and Rebecca to the fellowship of the church in a meaningful way.

Comments

It is obvious from this case that an active interventive mode was absolutely necessary. The pastor temporarily took responsibility for and control of the situation—he gave orders. Fortunately Rick trusted the pastor enough to follow these orders. Rick presented a good example of the lowered level of defensiveness and heightened psychological accessibility a person experiences in a crisis.

The pastor told Rick to call the fire department rather than an ambulance because he knew that in their city (and many others) the fire department automatically notifies the police and an ambulance in a suicide attempt. As a result three sources of help were soon rushing to the scene.

Finally, when the pastor asked questions about the attempted suicide, he was very specific: "With what?" "How much?" "How long ago?" It is always important in a suicidal crisis to get exact information and precise details.

A Case of Unwanted Pregnancy

Background

Marie Evans, thirty-five, an active member of First United Church, has been married for fifteen years to Frank Evans, a successful businessman. They have two children. Marie has been a part-time public school tutor for four years now and is looking forward to a full-time teaching position in the fall. Pastor Strand described the couple as "good solid church members who are always willing to do something extra if called upon."

The immediate situation

After a meeting with the junior-high church-school teachers broke up, Marie stayed behind. She was carrying on a casual conversation with the pastor about one of her students when she suddenly changed the tone of the conversation and said, "I've a bit of a problem." On their way to Pastor Strand's office she told him she had been to her doctor that morning and found she was seven weeks pregnant. She was less than thrilled by the idea and did not know what to do. She said her husband would go along with whatever she decided.

The precipitator of the crisis is obvious—an unwelcome pregnancy. None of the options—abortion, keeping the child, putting the child up for adoption—seemed good. Marie was at a loss about what to do.

Intervention

The pastor's relationship with Marie was already well-established. Before he asked how she saw the different alternatives, he helped her to boil the problem down. Though she felt some guilt about wanting an abortion, she definitely did not want the child. "It would be impossible for a married woman my age to give up a child for adoption," she said. The thought of abortion scared her, and she was also afraid of receiving a general anesthetic during the operation.

Pastor Strand happened to be on the board of the local Planned Parenthood Association and was able to pull from his files some literature on abortion. They reviewed the fairly detailed information. Marie was very interested and it was obvious to the pastor that her anxiety level was diminishing as she read. She found that a general anesthetic was not necessary and that no incision was required. "It doesn't sound as bad as I thought."

After they thoroughly discussed the alternatives, Marie said she felt pretty certain that she wanted the abortion. When Pastor Strand tried to probe into her feelings of guilt she said the information from Planned Parenthood had changed her mind, she felt assured that it would not be sinful, and she believed she would have no trouble with guilt. Pastor Strand told Marie she could either go to her own doctor, or the procedure could be arranged through Planned Parenthood. He suggested that she go home, talk it over with her husband, and pray about it before deciding.

At noon the next day Marie called Pastor Strand and said she and Frank had been up past midnight talking it over, and had decided definitely on an abortion. She would go to her own obstetrician. Pastor Strand suggested that they sit down and talk after the operation.

Follow-up

Two-and-a-half weeks later, Marie stopped by Pastor Strand's office to let him know that she had had the abortion and was feeling much better "now that the pressure is off." She did not feel any need to talk with him because she was not feeling the guilt she once had feared. She thanked him for his help, and information, and spiritual guidance.

Pastor Strand stopped over at the Evans's house a month later. During the conversation he asked how she felt now about the abortion, and she replied, "I made the right decision." She was feeling fine and was taking birth control pills, and she and Frank were talking about sterilization.

Comments

This was a fairly clear-cut and quite easily managed crisis for Pastor Strand. He already had a close relationship with

Marie and it took no effort to establish rapport with her. He also had little difficulty boiling down the problem. She was feeling a strong loss of freedom that would occur with another child, but also anxiety and guilt about having an abortion.

The pastor talked at some length with Marie about all three alternatives. After getting new information on abortion, she chose that option. With the information and discussion, both her guilt feelings and her anxiety were reduced. Pastor Strand suggested two different ways of having the abortion, and she chose the one that was most comfortable for her. Accurate information helped Marie Evans very much in resolving her crisis.

A Case of Lost Job Security

Background

Dennis Jackson, an eighteen-year-old junior college freshman, carries seventeen hours in school and works twenty hours a week for an employment agency. During high school he was very active in youth activities at church, and has known the youth pastor since early adolescence. He lives with his parents. Dennis is not certain he wants a bachelor's degree but he is interested in getting at least a two-year Associate of Arts degree and is taking general courses while deciding what he wants to do. He is considered by his youth pastor, Harold Rand, to be a well-adjusted person, mature beyond his years. Dennis is engaged to be married about a year after he receives his degree.

The immediate situation

Two weeks before Dennis sought the pastor's counsel, Mr. Carlton, office manager at the employment agency where Dennis works, terminated and went with another company. Now the former boss wanted Dennis to quit and come to work for him. Dennis was excited about this possibility at first, especially since he had begun to feel disappointed with his new office manager. Both Dennis's parents and his fiancée noticed that he was beginning to show anxiety and was expressing dislike for his new boss. At times he felt almost paranoid: his hours were being cut, he was being "put down," he wanted to quit. Mr. Carlton had made great promises concerning salary, travel allowance, vacation time, and future advancement, but when Dennis began getting serious about a possible change Mr. Carlton began to hedge a bit on some of these promises—though "they'd certainly be considered" when Dennis went full-time with the new company. Dennis had immediate reservations and quickly mounting feelings of uncertainty.

Dennis's crisis was stimulated by a loss of security. He felt he was no longer valued at his present job, and he also felt insecure about the promises growing vague when he pursued the new job offer. By the time he sought out Pastor Rand, Dennis was grieving over the loss of a secure and happy job situation. His coping methods appeared exhausted. He was requesting help of everyone, including his fiancée and parents, and was receiving conflicting advice.

Intervention

The night Dennis called Pastor Rand he had been struggling ineffectively all evening to write a term paper. He was so paralyzed by his indecision that it was affecting his schoolwork. Dennis told the pastor that he had problems and asked if they could sit down and talk as soon as possible. Pastor Rand arranged to see him between school and work the next day. When Dennis arrived in Pastor Rand's office he was clearly at loose ends. The pastor was quite passive, and allowed Dennis to tell him the whole story. Dennis was pleased with the good relationship he had with his former boss, Mr. Carlton, but he also raised some questions about the advisability of a change: Are conditions really that bad where he is presently employed? Were not his feelings of being "put down" simply a reaction to his new manager's insecurity? Would he be willing to talk with the branch manager about his relationship to the company? Dennis also had asked questions about the basic economics of the job change, especially the greater traveling distance.

After Dennis told his story Pastor Rand helped him to boil down the many facets of his problem. The consensual formulation which they arrived at was stated by the pastor: "What I hear you saying is that you feel paralyzed. You've had a good working relationship with your ex-boss, but since he left you've felt less happy, more anxious and concerned. You're in a dilemma, not knowing whether you should go to work for Mr. Carlton, given all the uncertainties and the greater distance to be traveled, or stay in your present job where you feel you might not be able to work with the new supervisor."

Dennis blurted out, "What do I do now?" Pastor Rand suggested that he see Mr. Warner, the general manager, and share his predicament with him before deciding what to do. He also suggested that Dennis obtain more data on his other job possibility, try to nail things down with his former employer, and come back in a couple days to discuss the new information.

Two days later when Dennis walked into Pastor Rand's office he was noticeably more relaxed. He had talked with Mr. Warner about his relationship with the new office manager. Mr. Warner had taken time to hear his story of dissatisfaction and understood the conflict of goals; he pointed out to Dennis that the present office manager was new, and was doubtless feeling somewhat threatened by a part-time worker who knew more than he did about the office, but he knew the office manager well and was certain this problem would pass in time. Mr. Warner added that a raise in salary for Dennis was in order, and that if Dennis would stay with them until he finished college there would definitely be a position for him—perhaps a managership at a branch office. Mr. Warner indicated that Dennis's first job at present, he felt, was to be a student.

Dennis also reported that he had checked once again

with his former boss and was not able to get any specific information. He now felt that the dilemma was definitely past and he would stay with his present employer. He was also excited about the small raise, felt more relaxed at work, and was already getting along better with his new office manager.

Follow-up

Pastor Rand reports that after several months Dennis appears to feel very secure with his work and happy with what he is doing. As the new office manager's security increased and Dennis's anxiety decreased, they began to work well together.

Comments

Pastor Rand deepened the already existing close relationship with Dennis by "attending" to him and by accurate listening. He interrupted only to clarify and to focus on Dennis's feelings and the issue at hand. He also helped Dennis to boil down the problem and the two together were able to develop a consensual formulation. Dennis knew he had a dilemma but he did not have enough data to make a decision concerning it. The pastor was fairly directive in suggesting what Dennis might do. It is possible that Dennis might have come up with the idea himself; nevertheless, he acted on Pastor Rand's suggestions and saw Mr. Warner, who not only gave him the information he needed but responded with warmth, interest, and support—both emotional and financial.

As a result of this crisis Dennis had several important learning experiences. First, he learned to trust significant others (such as pastor, parents, fiancée, and superiors at work) as resources in his life. Second, he developed increased skill at making decisions in a more mature way, and at avoiding paralysis of his coping methods. For Dennis the crisis had been a growth experience.

A Case of a Child's Reaction to a Move

Background

Pastor Sally Carpenter was an assistant minister in a large downtown church in the midwest. She was responsible for Christian education and also served as counselor for the church's parochial school.

Frequently in the morning Pastor Carpenter would walk through the halls of the school, greeting and being greeted by the children as they arrived. One Monday morning Patty, a six-year-old in the first grade, greeted Pastor Carpenter as usual and then added, "I have some bad news to tell you." When Pastor Carpenter asked what it was, Patty said: "My father has left home for a while." The pastor asked why, and Patty replied: "Because he has to work out of town."

Pastor Carpenter did not know Patty's parents well. Patty had two brothers attending the school—Matthew, eight, and Peter, eleven. She was shy, but always greeted Pastor Carpenter with a smile. Patty did not seem very upset that morning, and the pastor continued walking down the hall greeting other children.

The immediate situation

The next day, Patty's teacher came to Pastor Carpenter's office and related the following series of incidents: On the day before, Patty had also told him that her father had "gone away for a while." He passed it off since it did not seem to bother her, but that morning Patty asked the school secretary to call him out of the lounge before school started. Patty told her teacher that her father had come back home but "He doesn't love me anymore." When the teacher asked why she said that, Patty replied that her father had beaten her with his hand. The teacher brought her to the school nurse, who could find no signs of a beating. Throughout that morning Patty told the teacher one story after another —each more fantastic than the last: "The house burned down," "My mother almost died last night." Whenever the teacher discredited a story, Patty simply said she was kidding, and laughed.

This was atypical behavior for Patty who was generally a rather withdrawn child. Finally, just before lunch, Patty began to cry and said her stomach hurt and she felt sick. When the teacher asked if she wanted to go home, she screamed that she had no home and hated everybody, especially her daddy. The teacher brought Patty to the nurse's office and sought the assistance of Pastor Carpenter.

Intervention

After Pastor Carpenter and the teacher talked for a few minutes, they went down to the nurse's office to meet Patty. Pastor Carpenter related to Patty that her teacher had told her all the fantastic tales Patty had been telling, and asked "Is something bothering you?" Responding to the pastor's skill in empathetically talking with children, Patty finally opened up. During the past weekend her family had moved four streets away, from their apartment to a house. It appeared that no one in the family had taken the time to tell Patty anything about the move or why it was necessary. The loss of a familiar environment, friends, and a sense of security were too much for Patty to cope with. She viewed her father as the culprit, since he was the one who actually moved her things.

Patty was very close to her eight-year-old brother Matt, and the teacher suggested that Matt come to their class that afternoon. At the end of the day Peter came also. The brothers shared information about the move with Patty and the other children. The teacher also read stories about moving, and the entire class shared in Patty's experience. Patty discovered that two children in her class now lived a few houses away from her.

Meanwhile, Pastor Carpenter called the mother, explained the situation, and offered to stop by. The mother was too embarrassed by the messy house. Pastor Carpenter suggested then that the family, especially the father, talk with Patty about the move. The mother was responsive to the call and said they would talk that evening.

Follow-up

Pastor Carpenter was prepared to recommend play therapy for Patty if her problems continued, but when she checked back with Patty's teacher during the next few days he indicated that Patty was back to her old self. Patty's parents never called the pastor back, but at the parent-teacher conference three weeks later the teacher learned that they had talked at length that Tuesday evening at the supper table, and there did not seem to be any further problem for Patty.

Comments

Reviewing the case in light of the ABC method, it appears that Pastor Carpenter already had a relationship with Patty, though no more than a few words each day had passed between them. The pastor had a natural ability for relating with children. She boiled down Patty's problem: "You feel bad because you don't have your same house or your same friends anymore," and "You are mad at your daddy for making the move." To the latter statement Patty had blurted out her definite consensual formulation: "Yeah!"

The pastor and the teacher mutually took responsibility for forming a method of action. They set up situations where Patty could not only talk about her loss, but also receive the support of others. The teacher was very cooperative and therapeutic in his handling Patty. It appears that the parents, after becoming aware of Patty's problem, were also responsive to her feelings. The resolution of the crisis was worked out in a matter of hours, and Patty was back to her usual self thereafter.

5. The Church as Caring Community

"Let us give thanks to the God and Father of our Lord Jesus Christ, the merciful Father, the God from whom all help comes! He helps us in all our troubles, so that we are able to help those who have all kinds of troubles, using the same help that we ourselves have received from God." (2 Corinthians 1:3-4, Good News for Modern Man)

God's love for us is a prior condition for our loving others. The congregation can be an instrument through which God's love is translated to those in need. As a caring community, the church is especially well-suited for giving help to people in crisis.

The Church's Advantages

Thomas F. McGee, a mental health professional, believes there are four conditions which are essential for effective crisis intervention:* (1) Location. For crisis intervention to be effective, persons doing it must be involved with and located in a specific community; people in crisis—probably because of their paralysis, immobility, and confusion in thinking—rely upon those people or agencies which are readily accessible. (2) Availability. The person in crisis must be able to achieve contact with a helping person quickly, and during the period of crisis and not two or three weeks later; at moments of "heightened psychological accessibility" less counseling effort is required than after the "triangle" has tipped down again (see diagram 3 above). (3) Mobility. The mental health professional, who simply sits in a mental health center waiting for an individual in crisis to show up, is not able to take part in comprehensive crisis intervention. (4) Flexibility of procedure. Crisis intervention requires a variety of means and methods such as walk-in clinics, telephone calls, home visits, fifteen-minute supportive sessions, and use of paraprofessionals; it assumes the use of as many resources and support systems as possible. McGee's four considerations for good crisis intervention are frequently better met by the trained minister and congregation than by traditional mental health professionals.

One of the chief advantages of the church in crisis intervention is its location. It has for centuries been known as a place where individuals in distress can receive help.

Associated with the building is not only a minister but a total system of concerned people who can be mobilized in a short period of time to care for others. From the standpoint of crisis intervention this availability is a great advantage because people in crisis are generally able to see the minister or someone in the congregation within a day or two, if not immediately.

Ministers and laypersons in the church have a unique mobility. They make calls in homes, go to the scene of accidents and disasters, and visit people at work and in the hospital. The church's ministry is not viewed by the Christian community as being closed up in the sanctuary, but as being stretched and extended into the whole community. In fact, Christian fellowship never was limited to a church within a certain facility, but occurred "where two or three are gathered together."

It is noteworthy that mental health professionals are beginning to realize the necessity of flexibility in procedure. Many who thought they were very flexible, and considered themselves eclectic counselors, did most of their counseling within the four walls of an office for fifty-minute sessions of face-to-face contact. They rarely used methods of intervention that have been used historically by the congregation, such as home and hospital visits, the telephone, use of para-professionals and laypersons visiting those who are in difficulty, and incorporation of the needy person within a group of caring individuals—not to speak of worship services and Bible study and prayer groups to help meet spiritual needs.

I believe the purpose of the church is to increase and promote among all people love of God and of each other. The church has the task of making this love real and concrete to individuals, so that they can respond to it with increased love for God and for one another. The three traditional tasks of the church have been defined as kerygma (teaching and proclaiming the gospel), koinonia (fellowship), and diakonia (implementing the faith in Christian love and service). Crisis intervention fulfills all three forms of ministry. It proceeds primarily out of love and service (diakonia), but it also helps the person relate better with others as a part of the community of God (koinonia), and it facilitates new learning (kerygma) at a time when people are especially open to the gospel.

Counseling is, as Clinebell believes, "an instrument of renewal through reconciliation, helping to heal our estrangement from ourselves, our families, our fellow church members, from those outside the church, and from a growing relationship with God.* Crisis intervention, then, as we have stressed, is not just "Band-Aid therapy," nor is it just helping people to resolve their responses to a particular precipitator. It is also growth counseling, bringing renewal in a person's relationships with others and with God. It is within the local church fellowship, and not only through the minister, that persons can come to know and care for one another in a way that makes genuine Christian community possible and stretches the pastoral care ministry beyond what the pastor can do alone. When crises arise, the individuals are thus already in the middle of many resources they can use. Some of those who come to the minister from outside the church can be integrated into the Christian community as an additional resource for strength.

A Ministry for the Laity

The crisis care-giver does not have to be a minister or a mental health professional. The use of laypersons for crisis work is a natural approach to extending the network of care and counseling. Many crisis centers and suicide prevention agencies have used people such as housewives, attorneys, and construction workers who are trained specifically in crisis intervention methods. The pastor who would extend the caring ministry of the local parish beyond what "one person can accomplish" can enlist and train others to help in times of crisis.

One of the most effective ways of utilizing members of the congregation in crisis intervention work is to select a small cluster of lay visitors or "befrienders" and train them in intervention methods. Space here does not permit a detailed description of such a training program for befrienders;* however, it should involve not only cognitive input but also considerable role play, utilizing the ABC method of crisis intervention counseling. In this regard the minister can share typical cases for discussion in class and practice at home. Role play of telephone intervention can be done by having two people sit back-to-back to prevent them from relying on facial and nonverbal clues.

The crisis befrienders can function in various areas according to the needs of the individual congregation and minister, for example, in sick visitation, visiting after a death in a family, and visiting after a divorce. Crisis befrienders can also be trained in general pastoral care visitation; they can develop and use their skills for helping shut-ins and others who are lonely but not experiencing a crisis. In such situations the befrienders can function to share the minister's mammoth pastoral care responsibility, and to

establish on an ever-larger base of prior positive relationships—*A*—which is the foundation for intervention when
the need arises.

The befrienders have an ongoing need for supervision and
feedback. This occurs best in a group setting, except in
emergencies when the minister can consult with an individual befriender by phone or in person. Actually the training never ceases, but after the initial sessions it changes
from a weekly training program to biweekly or monthly
supervision and ad hoc consultation. Edwin Shneidman, in
discussing the training of paraprofessionals for crisis intervention, states, "What you need is a good heart, freedom
from proselytizing for your own private causes, supervised
training focused on crisis intervention, and a pinch of wis-
dom. . . . Three pre-conditions are essential: *careful* selec-
tion, *rigorous* training, and *continuous* ruthless supervision."*

If befrienders are to function successfully in congrega-
tions, it is essential that the ministers not be threatened by
people around them who are able to do certain pastoral
care tasks. If the minister feels comfortable in allowing befrienders to share in his or her pastoral care work, he or she
can then begin to educate the congregation in the concept
of ministry as a function of the total people of God. The
minister is not the sole possessor of the "keys to the king-
dom." There are, however, many crises when the pastor
must respond in person, such as at times of death or grave
illness. The efforts of the crisis befrienders do not necessarily cut down on the amount of pastoral care visitation
required of the minister—they may well increase it—but
they can ultimately offer the congregation a broader and
more effective visitation ministry.

There are a variety of ways for the pastor and congregation to be involved in a crisis work. A member of the congregation, for example, can help to encourage local crisis or
mental health centers to be effective and relevant to the
community. Church people can establish and man "hot

lines" or crisis intervention centers in communities where none exist. Ministers or members of the congregation can also serve on existing crisis lines or programs within the community which frequently need volunteer help.

The group effort of a caring congregation for those in crisis is an example of "convergence behavior," the kind that frequently occurs in connection with natural disasters, when there is an influx of people who are eager to help, looking for friends and relatives, or simply curious. Unfortunately "convergence behavior" rarely occurs in cases of emotional crisis, but in a congregation it can be fostered. This is what persons in crisis are unconsciously asking for. The helper must engage everyone he or she can find to meet the persons' needs and to reassure them that they have not been abandoned.

A sense of belonging and of fellowship with other Christians is important because in crisis we need other people. This can be facilitated through koinonia. The original Greek word *koinonia* suggests deep and genuine fellowship or sharing. In the New Testament Paul speaks of the participation and mutual fellowship among believers, stemming from the relationship of each individual believer with Christ. Koinonia is possible today among people who come together from all walks of life to share in one central concern.

Another dimension of koinonia is partnership: all Christians are partners in Christ. Even in the counseling relationship the helper and the counselee both give and receive from each other. Koinonia is always active, never passive or stagnant. It is spontaneous and uncontrived. It is not inward, but exists in relationships where sharing and reaching out occur, and it is vigorous and honest and can involve—even require—confrontation between people.

The potential for koinonia exists with all people. Out of it comes trust. As a result of it people will naturally go to each other for help in crises. This is of course an ideal, but whenever koinonia exists within a Christian community, pastoral care naturally becomes a function of the total congregation, thus increasing the chances for positive resolution and personal growth in crises.

Crisis intervention, whether undertaken by members of the congregation or the minister, or both, is a specialized form of ministry aimed at encountering and caring for those in crisis. It is not a panacea; not all people and situations will respond equally to crisis intervention. It is, nevertheless, a way in which the love of God can be expressed through the minister and the congregation to persons at their times of greatest need.

Notes

Page
3. *Cited in Wilbur Morley and Vivian B. Brown, "The Crisis Intervention Group: A Natural Mating or a Marriage of Convenience," *Psychotherapy: Theory, Research, and Practice* 6:1 (Winter, 1969), p. 1.

3. †Anton T. Boisen, *The Exploration of the Inner World* (New York: Harper & Row, 1961).

3. ‡Boisen, *Religion in Crisis and Custom* (New York: Harper & Row, 1955).

3. §Erich Lindemann, "Symptomatology and Management of Acute Grief," *Crisis Intervention: Selected Readings*, ed. Howard J. Parad (New York: Family Service Association of America, 1965), pp. 7–21.

4. *The "disease model," on the other hand, would assume that a breakdown of emotional function is a manifestation of an underlying disorder. The method of treatment based on the disease model is to "cure" psychological illness by changing the defective personality. Lindemann and Caplan, on the contrary, assume that a person's resistance to stress is finite, and that under some circumstances any individual's coping methods may become inadequate to sustain his or her psychological balance.

5. *For further information on developmental crisis, see Erik H. Erikson, *Childhood and Society*, 2d ed., rev. (New York: W. W. Norton & Co., 1964), especially pp. 247–74.

7. *Switzer, *The Minister as Crisis Counselor*, pp. 268–69.

8. *Clinebell, *Basic Types of Pastoral Counseling*, p. 158.

8. †LeRoy Aden, "Pastoral Counseling as Christian Perspective," *The Dialogue Between Theology and Psychology*, ed. Peter Homans (Chicago: University of Chicago Press, 1968), 3:174.

9. *Ibid.

9. †Carl G. Jung, *Modern Man in Search of a Soul* (London: Routledge & Kegan Paul, 1949), p. 264.

10. *Erich Fromm, *Man for Himself* (New York: Holt, Rinehart & Winston, 1947), p. 25.

10. †Viktor E. Frankl, *Man's Search for Meaning* (New York: Washington Square Press, 1963), p. 121.

13. *Lazarus, *Psychological Stress*, p. 153.

15. *Halpern, "Crisis Theory," p. 344.

15. †Ibid., p. 347.

17. *Edwin Shneidman, "Crisis Intervention: Some Thoughts and Perspectives," *Crisis Intervention*, ed. Gerald A. Specter and William L. Claiborn (New York: Behavioral Publications, 1973), p. 10.

19. *Quoted by Halpern, "Crisis Theory," p. 343.

19. †Ibid.

21. *Caplan, *Principles of Preventive Psychiatry*, p. 293.

21. †Ibid.

21. ‡Wilbur E. Morley, "Theory of Crisis Intervention," *Pastoral Psychology* 21:203 (April, 1970), p. 16.

22. *Stone, *Suicide and Grief*, pp. 69–70.

24. *Paul Tillich, quoted by Clinebell, *Pastoral Counseling*, p. 50.

28. *Gerald F. Jacobson, "Crisis Theory and Treatment Strategy: Some Socio-Cultural and Psychodynamic Considerations," *The Journal of Nervous and Mental Diseases* 141:2 (1965), pp. 214–15.

32. *Switzer, p. 54.

32. †Warren L. Jones, "The A-B-C Method of Crisis Management," *Mental Hygiene* (January, 1968), p. 87.

32. ‡Robert R. Carkhuff, *The Art of Helping*; idem, *Helping and Human Relations*, vols. 1 and 2 (New York: Holt, Rinehart & Winston, 1969); Allen E. Ivey, "Microcounseling and Attending Behavior," *Journal of Counseling Psychology* 15:5, pt. 2; and William Glasser, *Reality Therapy* (New York: Harper & Row, 1965).

38. *Rusk, "Crisis Psychiatry," p. 251.

47. *O. Hobart Mowrer, quoted in Clinebell, *Pastoral Counseling*, p. 171.

47. †Howard J. Clinebell, Jr., in the film, "New Approaches to Crisis Counseling," Pastoral Care in Crisis film series (Columbus, South Carolina: Community Mental Health Services, distributors).

51. *For further information concerning assessment of suicide lethality, see Stone, pp. 15–19.

53. *Clinebell, *Pastoral Counseling*, p. 177.

55. *Gerald Caplan, E. A. Mason, and D. M. Kaplan, "Four Studies of Crisis in Parents of Prematures," *Community Mental Health Journal* 1:2 (Summer, 1965), p. 151.

68. *Thomas F. McGee, "Some Basic Considerations in Crisis Intervention," *Community Mental Health Journal* 4 (1968), p. 323.

70. *Clinebell, *Pastoral Counseling*, p. 15.

71. *Helpful resources in. connection with conceiving a training program for lay befrienders are Howard J. Clinebell, Jr., *Growth Counseling: New Tools for Clergy and Laity*, Part 2, "Growth Counseling—Coping Constructively with Crises," Tape I—*Training Lay Persons for Caring* (Nashville: Abingdon Press, 1973-74); and Carkhuff, *The Art of Helping*.

72. *Shneidman, p. 11.

Annotated Bibliography

Caplan, Gerald. *Principles of Preventive Psychiatry*. New York: Basic Books, 1964. The second chapter, "A Conceptual Model for Primary Prevention," describes the characteristics of significant life crises and factors which influence their outcome.

Carkhuff, Robert R. *The Art of Helping*. Amherst, Mass.: Human Resource Development Press, 1972. Describes the attending, listening, and responding behaviors which are important components of the *A* and *B* phases of the ABC method.

————. *The Art of Problem Solving*. Amherst, Mass.: Human Resource Development Press, 1973. Contains a more complete exposition of how a helper can do problem solving with a client (*C* of the ABC method).

Clinebell, Howard J., Jr. *Basic Types of Pastoral Counseling*. Nashville: Abingdon Press, 1966. Chapter 9 suggests several different approaches to crisis counseling.

Farberow, Norman L.; Heilig, Samuel M.; and Litman, Robert E. *Techniques in Crisis Intervention: A Training Manual*. Los Angeles: Suicide Prevention Center, Inc., 1968. A short but valuable guide to counseling an individual who is considering suicide.

Halpern, Howard A. "Crisis Theory: A Definitional Study." *Community Mental Health Journal* 9, no. 4 (Winter, 1973):342–49. Reformulates crisis in terms of a cognitive model or theory, correlating crisis behaviors with crisis-producing situations and reduced defensiveness on the part of persons in crisis.

Jackson, Edgar N. *Coping with the Crises in Your Life.* New York: Hawthorn Books, 1974. Written for the general public, it deals with both developmental and situational crises.

Lazarus, Richard S. *Psychological Stress and the Coping Process.* New York: McGraw-Hill, 1966. A ponderous but valuable volume which details a cognativist view of stress; discusses primary and secondary appraisal of perceived threat.

Oates, Wayne E. *Pastoral Care in Crucial Human Situations.* Valley Forge, Pa.: Judson Press, 1969. A helpful book which deals with such crucial concerns as mentally retarded children, chronically ill persons, and children with cancer.

Parad, Howard J., ed. *Crisis Intervention: Selected Readings.* New York: Family Service Association of America, 1965. Twenty-nine chapters of varying quality, two of the more valuable being Lindemann's classic article on grief and Hill's chapter on crisis in the family.

Pastoral Psychology 21 (April, 1970):203. The entire issue of this journal is devoted to the minister and crisis intervention; included are articles by Gerald Jacobson ("Crisis Intervention from the Viewpoint of the Mental Health Professional"), Wilbur Morley ("Theory of Crisis Intervention"), and David K. Switzer ("Crisis Intervention Techniques for the Minister").

Pretzel, Paul W. "An Introduction to Crisis Counseling: Making the Best Use of the Dangerous Opportunity." *Research and Pupil Personnel Services Newsletter* 7, no. 3 (March 13, 1970): Los Angeles School System, 406. A short, clear, and concise description of crisis intervention counseling, written for people who are not mental health professionals.

Rusk, Thomas N. "Opportunity and Technique in Crisis Psychiatry." *Comprehensive Psychiatry* 12 (May, 1971).

Discusses a number of basic issues of crisis intervention, including the concept of consensual formulation.

Specter, Gerald A., and Claiborn, William L., eds. *Crisis Intervention.* New York: Behavioral Publications, 1973. An edited volume including especially valuable articles by Shneidman, Levy, Korner, and Sebolt.

Stone, Howard W. *Suicide and Grief.* Philadelphia: Fortress Press, 1972. Although focusing mainly on the grief occurring after a suicide, it discusses crisis intervention and the management of a person who is threatening suicide.

Strickler, Martin, and La Sor, Betsy. "The Concept of Loss in Crisis Intervention." *Mental Hygiene* 54, no. 2 (April, 1970):301–5. Believing *loss* is basic in all crisis situations, the authors examine three fundamental adult losses: self-esteem, sexual role mastery, and nurturing.

Switzer, David K. *The Minister as Crisis Counselor.* New York: Abingdon Press, 1974. An excellent volume covering all aspects of a pastor's intervention in the crises of his parishioners.

Taplin, Julian R. "Crisis Theory: Critique and Reformulation." *Community Mental Health Journal* 7, no. 1 (1971): 13–23. A good attempt at reformulating crisis theory in less psychoanalytic constructs; presents eight basic facets of a crisis.

Whitlock, Glenn E. *Preventive Psychology and the Church.* Philadelphia: Westminster Press, 1973. The third part of this book on preventative pastoral care discusses the pastor's use of crisis intervention.